The Redhill Story

NIGEL DUNNE

Nigel Dunne

D. CANNING, REDHILL 150
1994

Published by D. Canning, REDHILL 150, 77 Rathgar Close, Whitebushes Estate, Redhill, Surrey RH1 5LR.

Copyright Nigel Dunne 1994

ISBN 0 9523820 0 8.

Printed in UK by Swiftprint, Hockley Industrial Centre, Redhill. Typesetting by Steve Newton, for and on behalf of Swiftprint.

Cover courtesy John Capon

All rights reserved. No part of this book may be reproduced or transmitted in any form or by any means, electronic or mechanical, including photocopy or any information storage and retrieval system without permission in writing from the publisher.

THE REDHILL STORY

CONTENTS

PREFACE
PROLOGUE
CHAPTER 1 .... REDEHELDE
CHAPTER 2 .... REIGATE FOREIGN
CHAPTER 3 .... THE RAILWAYMAN COMETH
CHAPTER 4 .... WARWICK TOWN
CHAPTER 5 .... THE ROOTS OF GROWTH
CHAPTER 6 .... THE VICTORIAN LEGACY
CHAPTER 7 .... A QUICKENING TEMPO
CHAPTER 8 .... LAUGHTER AND TEARS
CHAPTER 9 .... NO SANCTUARY FROM ABOVE
CHAPTER 10 .... A TOWN OF CHANGE
CHAPTER 11 .... TOWARDS THE MILLENNIUM
APPENDIX 1 .... REDHILL SNIPPETS
APPENDIX 2 .... THE OLD MILL
APPENDIX 3 .... EARLSWOOD VILLAGE
ACKNOWLEDGEMENTS
BIBLIOGRAPHY
ABOUT THE AUTHOR

PREFACE

When Danny Canning and his REDHILL 150 committee asked me if I would write a history of the town, I was of course delighted but at the same time slightly apprehensive. Delighted, because it was an opportunity to extend the knowledge and interest I had gained from researching my previous book. ARTHUR, which I wrote in 1989, was basically a biography but he was an Earlswood man and as such this had sent me delving into Redhill's history. As I have since discovered, I only "scratched at the surface" but as a social historian it was inevitable that I wanted to know more.

That I was slightly apprehensive of the task is perhaps an understatement, given the time restraints and the understanding that 150 years had to be researched, collated and written within them. In addition, there were other factors such as the nature and depth of the content, selection of illustrations, design, layout and printing. A daunting task perhaps but a wonderful opportunity to learn more about this fascinating town. There was also the incentive that no history of Redhill itself had been written before.

First of all THE REDHILL STORY is not a definitive history; neither is it a detailed chronological list of political, council and other historical data. It is, rather, one story of the social and business life of the town and its people. I emphasise one story, because in 150 years of existence, there must be thousands of stories that could be written about Redhill. It is a story, too, of the people who came to work and live here; the most important element, people, without whom there would be no town.

The 150th anniversary which we are celebrating this year, is the completion of the railway station and the birth of the embryo town of Warwick as it was then known. Though the arrival of the railways was the principal cause of the development of the town, it can be said that the opening up of the Redhill district effectively dates from the construction of the turnpike road to Brighton in 1816. Prior to this time the district, which was then known as Reigate Foreign, was comprised of several small hamlets. How they would have developed had the railways been built elsewhere is pure conjecture and conjecture has no place in this story. But the hamlets themselves do have a place, for they are now all part of Redhill and the historical link with the past.

Prior to the arrival of the railways the majority of local industries were agricultural. Around the 'pocket' communities of Linkfield Street, Wiggie, Hooley, Meadvale and Little London (St. Johns), there were several sizeable farms attached to the submanors. Further afield there were others and most tenants grew crops for their own use. But the single most important industry was Fullers Earth, which had been dug out for centuries between Redstone Hill and Bletchingley. In fact it was the Romans who had introduced the industry into Britain. Another industry was brickmaking, the clay of the Weald providing the right components. At Linkfield Street, the tannery had been the most prominent in the area for centuries and continued in business well into the present century. The hamlets were largely self-sufficient and had little contact with Reigate, other than paying their rents to the Lord of the Manor.

There is no doubt that the subsequent arrival of the railways and the rapid development of Redhill made a dramatic impact on these rural communities. Life would never be the same again, a phrase used many times throughout this story. But the tranquillity of village life did continue for many years, as T.R. Hooper discovered and dramatically described in 1854.

THE REDHILL STORY is, I suppose, a presentation of historical snapshots of social and business life, people and events, along a journey that starts in the primitive days of Stoneage man. Inevitably some events and aspects of town life have been excluded, not because they were unimportant, but rather the sheer impossibility of including everything.

Amongst the appendices at the end of this book is a map and description of the businesses operating in Earlswood around 1923. I have not singled out Earlswood for any particular reason, other than a few years ago I researched its history in some depth. I have included it here because it is, in a way, a snapshot in time of another era. A time when village life really was village life; when people like Arthur King and his fellow villagers rarely went to town to shop, because the village provided everything.

THE REDHILL STORY will, I hope, give the present generation and those that follow some idea of the town's origins and the events which have shaped its growth. But of more importance it is a story of the townsfolk themselves, who in one way or another have determined the history of their town. It is also a story of us who live here now, for we are the present-day history-makers. Not just the present-day builders and creators of the material town, but the guardians of its character and spirit. Perhaps unconsciously we may have already achieved both, when one resident recently remarked;

> "The Harlequin Theatre was what Redhill needed for years. It has, I think, become the soul of the town".

Let tomorrow's history-makers be the judges.

Nigel Dunne
Redhill
June 1994

PROLOGUE

Every story must have a beginning.

In fiction this is relatively easy, but in the context of history the beginning can be more complex. Certainly this must be true of a town, for when does a town become a town? Is it a gradual process over centuries, or is the cause as a result of a major event?

There are of course a variety of answers. A sleepy village finds itself with a new industry. This has the effect of creating new jobs, increasing the population and building new homes. This in time has a snowball effect as other businesses and people arrive. Eventually the village becomes a town. Perhaps this is a rather simplistic view, but a major event does have this effect and the end result is expansion. In a sense this is how Redhill the town was born. This is where the story could start, with the arrival of the railways and the building of the station. But to do so would be to exclude Redhill the district, or Reigate Foreign as it was called well into the nineteenth centry. For it is here that the origins of the town lie; in the pocket communities of Linkfield Street, Hooley, Wiggy, Meadvale and Little London, which were all part of Reigate Foreign.

This then is where the story will begin.

****

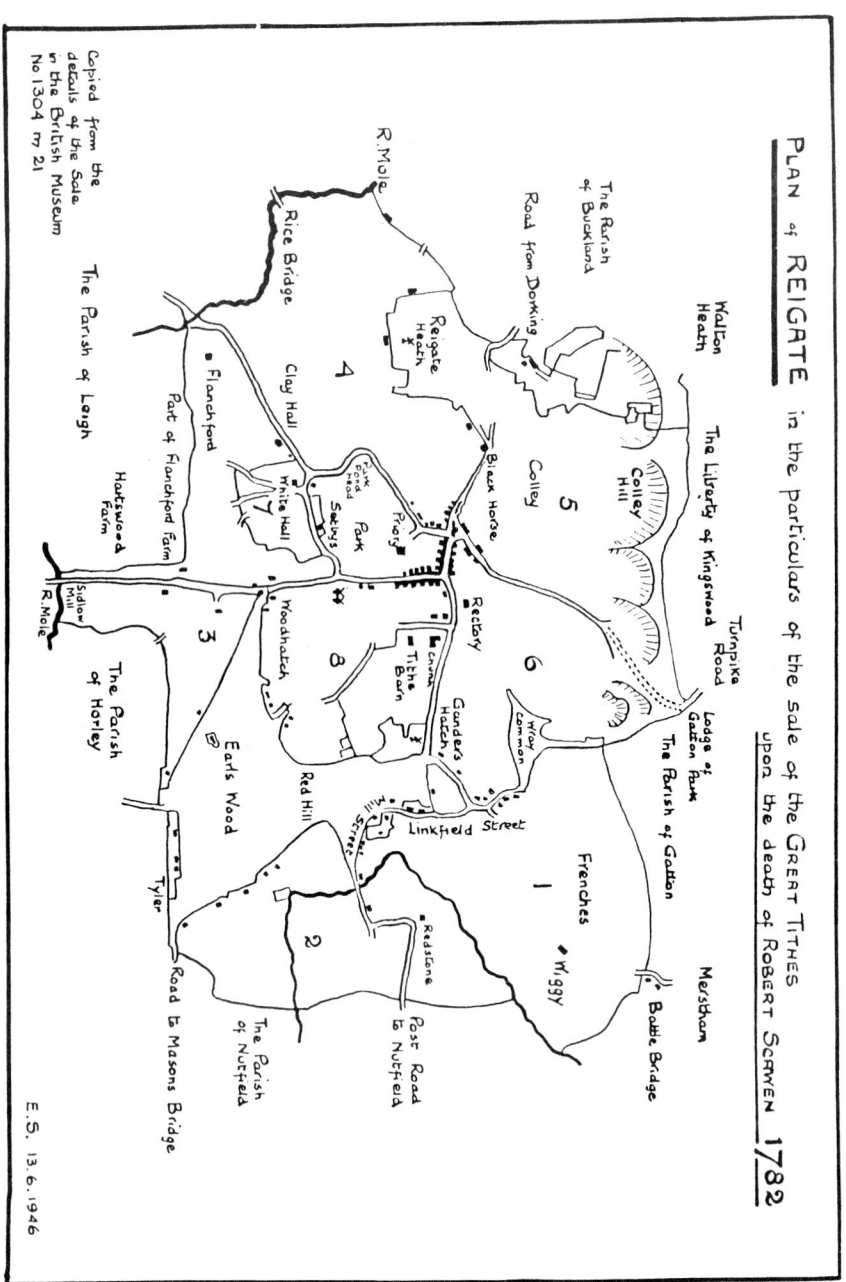

Chapter 1
REDEHELDE

There appears to be little doubt that a Stoneage settlement existed in the Vale of Holmesdale, which included the general area of Reigate, Redhill and Merstham. In the Redhill area early man would have had the convenience of a ready water supply, since the brook is considered to have been deeper and wider than it is today. The main settlement lay between the slopes of Redstone Hill and Red Hill, which then stretched from Garlands Road to its peak on the Common. Other mini-settlements existed near the brook at Hooley and on the slopes of Redstone Hill, to the east of the railway station site. In many ways it was an ideal location for these early settlers, with the heavily forested Earlswood area offering good hunting-grounds. Closer at hand the low-lying marshes through which the brook flowed, were abundant with ducks, geese, snipe and other wild life. Further north the Downs provided the hunters with an ample supply of flints for their implements and weapons.

All that remains of this early colony is the evidence of their tools and weapons, for no structures have been found. In fact no structural remains have been found anywhere in Britain, of what has become known as the Mesolithic Period c. 8000-3000 BC. But the "finds" in Redhill were considered significant, even though they gave little information about their owners. Between 1847 and 1860 John Shelley collected thousands of flint flakes, cores, saws and a leaf-shaped arrowhead from sandy soil near the station. Most were found in a field next to the railway line on the east side of Ladbroke Road. Some years later other artifacts were found by Sydney Webb of Redstone Manor, dating from the Bronze Age. These were discovered north-east of the station in an area described at the time as, "the broad valley watered by the nameless stream, which flows southward through the bold gap in the greensand ridge, now occupied by Redhill town and joins the river Mole at Sidlow Bridge".

Other discoveries followed. In 1902 a double-headed flint axe was unearthed in Hillfield Road, while a short distance away a barbed arrowhead and knife were dug up in a garden on the Hooley Mead Estate in Earlswood.

And there the legacies of Mesolithic Man and his successor Neolithic Man end, offering no further clues of how they lived. Presumably their Stone and Bronze Age lives continued largely unaffected for many centuries, at least until the arrival of the Romans in 43 BC. Not that there is much evidence of Roman dwellings either, though the foundations of what may have been a villa were found on the east side of Earlswood Common. Certainly no attempt was made to build villas in the marshes of Redhill, though it appears they had a look at the possibility, for many years later a silver coin of the emperor Antonius Pius, c. 44BC, was unearthed at the corner of Sincots Road and Grove Road.

But if the marshes were not for them, the red clay of the surrounding hills most certainly was. For in it they recognised the properties essential for cleansing woollen cloth. It was a discovery which was to lead to a variety of uses over the next two thousand years, as well as providing local employment. The Romans also discovered that the principal sources of the clay extended from Redstone Hill to the west side of Bletchingley. Certainly a vast area by their standards and one which would meet their needs for a considerable time. And of course future generations, but then they could not possibly have foreseen that, or the varied uses that Fullers Earth would provide. Not that they called it Fullers Earth of course, but their own latin words are very similar; "Fullonicae", being the laundry areas of Roman villas and "Terra", meaning earth. The industry thrived during the middle ages, but then declined when soap was introduced for the fulling of cloth in the last century. However this decline was relatively brief, when it was discovered Fullers Earth could be used for refining lard substitutes. Today, the industry now run by Laporte Earths has diverse uses in the fields of oil refining, moulding sands and civil engineering. An important range of absorbents is also produced, including litter for cats and other pets.

The departute of the Romans from Britain around 410 AD was followed by the Anglo-Saxon 'barbarians' who, over the ensuing centuries, settled in Merstham and the neighbouring area. They rapidly became domesticated, centring their lives around the villages and churches they built. But the peace of this domestic scene was rudely interrupted in the 9th century by the Danish invasion. According to an ancient legend, some of their number made their way to Merstham and were set upon by the women of Gatton and slaughtered. Whether this event did take place at Battlebridge is debatable, but apparently the women used every kind of agricultural tool to perform the deed. Where their menfolk were at the time is not recorded. Though documentation of the period is scant and tales unreliable, the Manor of Gatton certainly existed at the time. And so presumably did the fields of Gatton where the slaughter took place, for ancient folklore records that 'Danewort has grown and thrived there, from the Danish blood which seaped into the ground'.

With the departure of the invaders life returned to normal. To the south a small community established itself at Petridge Wood which they called Pedasridge. Like Earlswood it was heavily wooded with oak and beach trees, part of the forests that swept southwards dividing Surrey from Sussex. By 1243 the wood had come to be pronounced Pederig, when reference was made to the cutting down of "many oaks". This devastation continued throughout the reign of Charles the first, as it did elsewhere in the county.

By 1300 a number of villages had established themselves as thriving and self-sufficient communities. But the marshlands between Redstone and Red Hill remained uninhabited, except for the movements of wildlife and the sounds of the gurgling brook. Above on the hills, however, there were signs of life, as a rough track was hacked out as a route from Nutfield to Reigate. And with it, too, came a new name for the second hill, Redehelde.

Chapter Two
REIGATE FOREIGN

Redehelde in 1300, only referred to the wooded red hill over which the medieval highway crossed to Reigate. It was of course an appropriate name in view of the red sandy soil which covered its slopes. But, like the neighbouring manor houses and hamlets, various spellings and pronunciations of the name have occurred over the centuries. By 1588 it was known as Redd Hyll and during the Civil War was also referred to as Red Hill in Reigate, or more correctly Reygate. At the same time Merstham was spelt Mestham, though in earlier years the present day spelling was in common use. The changes were due to different pronunciations over periods of time. And it is quite conceivable that today's sounding of the name by some members of the community, viz MERSTRUM, could herald a future change! The other pocket communities also underwent changes with Hooley being known at different times as, Holeghc - Houleigh - Howleigh and Houghley.

In Reigate Foreign, development of the separate communities during the Middle Ages was gradual and only relevant to the manor houses which controlled them. But the manor houses were effectively sub-manors, paying tithes or rents to the Lord of the Manor at Reigate. Within Reigate Foreign these included Hooleigh, Redstone, Linkfield and Frenches, of which the homestead of Wiggey was part. All of these sub-manors and their tenants enjoyed a generally peaceful existence within the rural Vale of Holmesdale. It was a medieval backwater with little outside contact and one which the historian Camden referred to as;

"The Vale of Holmsdall
Never wonne ne never shall".

In 1622 a survey reported;

"There are divers pettie manors within this manor, viz,the Manor of Redstone, holden by George Husseye, Gent; the Manor of Frenches held by Edward Drake, Gent...which are holden over to this Manor of Reigate".

Edward's father Henry, who had been a close relative of Sir Francis Drake, died in 1609 and was buried in Reigate Parish Church. The lands of the estate were extensive and largely used for farming purposes around the homestead of Wiggey, which at that time was occupied by Richard Ace. Here both meadow and arable land at Broadmeade and Bakers Brooke, were cultivated to the very edges of the marshes to the east and south. Above them the Manor of Redstone nestled in different terrain amidst leafy trees and evergreen shrubs. Over the years there had been numerous owners since John de Montford had occupied the mansion in 1292. But now it was in the hands of the Husseye or Hussee family, whose relative John had bought it in 1583 from one John Mitchell who;

> "In consideration and etc did sell unto John Hussee, all the Manor of Redstone in the Parish of Reigate in the county of Surrey , and all the houses, barns, stables, yards, casements and backsides, together with the scyte of the same Manor. And all lands meadows, pastures, woods, waters, wastegrounds, ways, warrens, fishings, rents, reversions and services and all courts, and profits of courts, liberties, preheminencies, commodities, profits, and advantages whatsoever part, parcel or member, of the same Manor or unto the same belonging. And all other lands, tenements and hereditaments whatsoever of the said John Mitchell, situate, lying, and being in Reigate aforesaid, in the County of Surrey".

Among the deeds of the estate was the following licence;

> "AGREEMENT indorsed on said assignment to said Peyto, his heirs and assigns, the use in Common with said Sir Evelyn, his exors, admors., assigns of the penstock and wears on the brook, and liberty of making a channell for a new stream through the lower part of the mill grove, and the horseleaze next the brook, about four rod, to pen or flow the water, to bring out of the old stream into such new stream to be cut to Carry

> the same into Doweshill, for the use of a watermill then to be erected in Doweshill, and for the purpose to make bays, bank, and mounds against the old stream. And the liberty and use of the waste ground between such new stream and the bank of Redstone mead, to pass and repass in and through the same".

The exact location of Doweshill is not recorded but the old stream refers to the Redhill brook. Whether a watermill was built is unknown but one did exist in later years off Hooley Lane and was immortalised in a poem by Eliza Cook.

In the late sixteen hundreds Redstone Manor passed to Sir George Colebrook of Gatton. By 1786 it was up for sale again as a manor,

> "with court-baron, quit rents, reliefs and heriots, an elegant mansion, garden, orchard and 109 acres 3 roods 1 pole of land, of which 12 acres are copyhold, held of the Manor of Reigate".

The adjacent manor house of Howleigh was in a low-lying marshy area which must have been extremely damp. The estate extended over most of present-day Earlswood and included the higher ground of Woodlands Road and Mill Street. The first mention of the manor was in 1390 during the reign of Richard II, when a bailiff reported that,

> "Holeghc was occupied by the same owner as Flanchford".

This gentleman was John de Brewes of whom little is known. By 1551 the manor had passed to William, Lord Howard of Effingham by the decree of Edward the sixth. Since the Howards owned many properties in England, it is unlikely that he spent any length of time here. His son Charles who succeeded to the estate in 1581, was created Earl of Nottingham in 1596, as reward for his services in capturing Cadiz from the Spanish. At the time the estate was described as including;

> "The old park called Reygate Park and two parcels of meadow ground called Howleigh Meade and Howleigh Garden, adjoining to the lands called Woodlands and the Brooke there on the west part".

Upon his death Howleigh passed from the Howards, when his second wife married William Monson who was later created Lord Monson and

Viscount Castlemaine in Ireland. In 1752 the estate was purchased by the Reigate tanner John Burt, but its days as a residence were numbered. After passing to Charles, Lord Somers the last owner, a Mr Roberts, sold it to the London, Brighton and South Coast Railway in 1838.

So much for the Lords and sub-Lords, but what of the poor peasant folk themselves while their masters were buying and selling properties? Most were unaffected by changes of ownership, as they were virtually tied to the manor for life and it mattered little who was their master. Others who were not employed on the manor estates found work at the tanneries, mills and at Fullers Earth. Here in the sixteen hundreds business was apparently very prosperous and records show that the earth sold at 4d a sack or six shillings by the load. But working conditions left much to be desired, as John Aubrey the historian of the period noted.

> "The Place is very narrow and small, from whence this Earth is dug and, as Sir Cyrill Wych informs me, Tempests are frequent here".

If working conditions were bad, many of the wretched dwellings the peasants lived in were even worse. And these conditions of squalor were particularly bad in Reigate, where rats and other vermin ran rife in the houses and streets. A natural breeding-ground for a serious epidemic, which was not long in coming, swept down from the filth of London in 1665. Though the Black Death accounted for only 107 deaths in the Parish, this number represented a high percentage of the population. Most of the deaths were in the town, leaving the rural communities largely unaffected.

Admittedly the rural cottages were primitive but the country folk at least had the benefit of space and fresh air. And in particular the folk who lived and worked on the Common lands of Earlswood, or Aleswood as it was then known. Here they worked as pottery-makers, using the Weald clay which surrounded them. It was a thriving industry with kilns stretching from Meadvale to Kiln Brow in the south-east. Several examples of their products have been unearthed, including tiles and a jug which was found on the site of the old golf clubhouse in Common Road.

Like other country people they farmed their meagre patches of land to feed themselves and pay their tithes. But they were not averse to poaching or fishing in the New Pond to the west, which had been a ready source of supply since 1363. Apparently this illegal fishing had little effect on the fish population, for a survey in 1700 described the lower lake as "a long pond well stored with ffish". But the other sources of wildlife food were becoming scarce, as the policy of tree-cutting continued unabated in the woods of Earlswood and Petridge. In fact, if anything, the tree-cutting intensified with the demands for ships' masts. At first this did not affect the activities of the local tenants, who continued their practice of "shaking and breaking" the trees for acorns. But in 1619 the order was made;

"that if any do hereafter break any trees for acorns
or gather any acorns in any of the said woods or
commons, they shall forfeit 3s.6d for every offence".

Soon afterwards at the next court session in Reigate, several tenants were reported for breach of the order and fined the full sum. But the fines apparently did not deter others until 1635, when Lord Monson had most of the trees cut down "for reasons not recorded". This move was resented by the local people who tried to stop him, but without success. Their resentment later turned to annoyance when he introduced rabbits which damaged their crops. A clear example of the power of the Manor.

Though there were a number of dwellings and pottery businesses scattered over the Common, there were few clusters of houses which could be called hamlets. At St. Johns, then known as Little London, there were several cottages around the Plough Inn which stood beside a rough track that led from the top of White Post Hill and across the Common to Salfords. At Mead Hole (Meadvale) there were more cottages close to the tannery and the kilns but few beyond until another rough track reached Woodhatch and the road south from Reigate. Though it contained only a small community, Woodhatch was a compulsory stopping place with its own tollgate and keeper's cottage. In 1623 the Angel across the road was described as "the Bowling Alley lying before the gate of the Tenement called Woodhatch". Parts of the present building date from that time, but it did not become an inn until the seventeen hundreds when it was known as The White Horse.

By the middle of the century after a period of decadence, which resulted in the execution of Charles I, a Commonwealth government was established in London with Oliver Cromwell as Lord Protector. The event marked the beginning of the English Civil War, as bands of Royalists took to various parts of the country. Though no major battles took place in the Reygate Hundred, several skirmishes did take place on Red Hill with mixed results. In one encounter near Ridgeway Road, the Royalists were the victors but, since parliament troops were in control of Reigate, they were forced to retreat to Dorking.

In 1659 the Royalists were again summoned to a rendezvous on Red Hill in a further attempt at insurrection. But this time the Government were informed of the plot. Two letters were sent to Major Audely, who was in charge of the Government troops at Reigate, from General Fleetwood. The first letter instructed him that two Troops to assist Colonel Hacker's regiment were to be at, "Redd Hill tomorrow by break of day". The second must have created a certain amount of confusion.

"FOR MAIOR AUDLY AT RIGAYT

Ma: Audly. The Counsell not understanding that there was 2 Redd Hil's in Surrey, and not knowing which of the Redd Hills is the place designed by the Enimy for a Rendesvouze, and orders being issued out upon the presumption that there was but one Redd Hill, they therefore think fit that the 2 Troopes from hence should goe to the Redd Hill by Cobham, and the party with You to the Redd Hill by Rigayt, and if you think there is a gathering together of the Enimy about that Place, you are to send to the other Redd Hill to Mr Hubbert for assistance, and accordingly he is to correspond with you. We are apt to think the Enimy is mistaken of the place, as well as we, and we hope there may be a Providence in the mistake,
Your affectionate friend and general,
Charles Fleetwood
*You are to be at one of the clock in the morning upon Redd Hill".

Providence there most surely was, but not with the best results for the Royalists, as most of them were captured and the rest put to flight.

These incidents had little effect on the lives of the inhabitants of Reigate Foreign, though the dwellers in Linkfield Street were rather too close for comfort. However, the hostelry of the White Lion probably benefited after the second skirmish, for it was well known as "the principal inn between Croydon and Sussex". Dating from Medieval times, it is today generally considered the oldest pub in the district which has continuously served drink and never closed. Certainly it had a prominent position beside the "ancient highway", that brought coaches and other traffic past its doors. Like most other main roads the surface was rutted and barely passable in wet weather. But it did serve as the main east to west route, where at the bottom it branched left to Reigate. At this junction which was to become known as Linkfield Corner, the other fork travelled east past the manor house and along Linkfield Lane to Frenches. From here the road became little more than a dirt track until it had passed through Battlebridge and reached Merstham.

By the end of the century Linkfield Street had assumed some importance besides its famous coaching inn. This was due to the tanyard further down the road which had become the largest in the area. Every week it sent a wagon full of leather to London, which on the return journey brought back a variety of goods including coal. In the immediate vicinity several farms were dotted around including a large one at High Trees, Fengates across the road from the White Lion and another at Shaw's Corner or Ganders Hatch as it was then called. Here, on the rising ground to the west, was the newly built Blackborough Mill with its great sails, an imposing landmark for miles around. It stood where the top of Millway is today and for nearly two hundred years provided employment for a great many people. When it was demolished in 1938, an inscription on one of the old beams gave the date as 1736, though the earliest record of its existence was in 1700.

The seventeen hundreds seem to have been an era of highway robberies, rape, murder and a host of other offences. The Assizes in Reigate appeared to be in continuous session though, apart from the non-payment of rents, most of the good citizens of Reigate Foreign were law-abiding. But not so one Richard Rodes, an oatmeal maker of Reigate. For having "kept" a woman as a housekeeper for some years, he murdered her one night and buried the body in the garden. Whereupon he fled to Ireland and became a waiter at an inn. After the body was discovered, the authorities advertised for him in a newspaper. A gentleman staying at the inn read the report and feeling the waiter answered the description, asked him to write his name. Upon writing

"Richard Rodes" he was arrested and confessing to the crime, brought to England for trial. At Reigate Assizes he was found guilty and hanged from a tree outside his house. His body was then trussed up in chains on Red Hill Common but was taken away the same night.

Many years later near the Workhouse, a man named Burt was digging up a tree when he came upon the bones of a man. The general opinion at the time was that these were the remains of the murderer Rodes and the body buried there by the people of the Workhouse. Burying bodies on the Commons was probably a regular occurance, but only after permission was granted. This had been the case in 1593 when a glassman died on Redhill Common and was buried there "by consent of the Parish".

But the Parish of Reigate had other problems and none more urgent than the growing numbers of destitute people. There was already one poor house or workhouse at Shaw's Corner, which had been there since 1720. For many years the road beside it was known as Workhouse Lane until, in 1863, it changed to Hatchlands after an old farm in the area. The reason the workhouse was located here was because it was isolated and away from Reigate town, where it was not wanted. Better to be heard of but not seen by the gentlefolk, as they went about their business. But the Parish agreed a second workhouse was needed and turned to Lord Somers of the Manor of Reigate for help. The obliging Lord had the very place for it and by a deed dated 11th May 1793, consented to the,

"enclosing of ten acres of land lying at a place called Broad Plain, being on the south part of Red Hill near Little London, for the purpose of building a Poor House or Workhouse".

The new workhouse would not only serve Reigate but also Reigate Foreign, Horley, Nutfield and Headley. Accordingly, for administration purposes and the welfare "of the publick as a whole", the joint parishes formed themselves into a Poor Law Union. Building began immediately and when the new house was completed in 1794, it was described as "a large fair brick building". Within a short time the inmates were hard at work and a woollen industry was set up for the manufacture of blankets, rugs and wagon tilts.

With the new workhouse established the lords and ladies could sit back and relax, no longer faced with the problem of wandering vagrants and beggars. Not that George Colebrook of Gatton was in the habit of relaxing, for he had more important matters of state to look after. As local member of Parliament for the 'Borough' of Gatton, he was carrying on a notorious role that had been granted to John Timperley by Henry VI. This gentleman, having 'done great services to the crown', had been honoured by the king to represent the borough in Parliament. It was the start of what was to become known as one of the most notorious and undemocratic Rotten Boroughs in England. But in those early days it probably mattered little, as each successive owner was automatically elected an MP.

After Timperley, Gatton passed to the Copley family in the early fifteen hundreds. On his death in 1704, Thomas Turgis left his estate to William Newland his grand-nephew, who continued to live there and carry out his 'Borough' duties until he died in 1738. George Colebrook, who inherited Gatton from his brother, may well have been an able administrator but he had grandiose ideas which he put into practice. One of them was in the form of the folly or temple he built in the grounds of Gatton. This became known as Gatton Town Hall and it was here that the 'elections' for the borough were held. By now parliamentary seats like Gatton had become scandals, with bribery and corruption rife. Throughout the country Rotten Borough MPs resigned in favour of their friends, when they quite often found they had already been elected to other constituencies. It was a deplorable state of affairs, but not one that was to be seriously addressed until a more democratic electoral system was introduced in the nineteenth century.

But none of these "rotten happenings" worried Sir Evlyn Alston at Redstone Manor. In fact it was unlikely that he was even aware of them, for according to William Ridgeway in his HISTORY OF REIGATE,

> "He came in his coach to it and lived at it some years until he had spent all his fortune. He used frequently to come to the town and get tipsy, and have music to play him all the way home - until he had nothing to support himself and family. The public houses that he used would not credit him with a pint of beer after he had spent all".

And these hostelries undoubtedly included his local, the recently opened Marquis of Granby and the Red Lion at Linkfield Corner. But his coachman would also have brought him past the White Lion and its tempting ales. For it was a popular stopover for travellers and in particular those who had journeyed some distance, as had a certain horseman many years before.

There have been many stories associated with the inn, but none so strange as the one about this weary horseman who had travelled from Sussex and decided to stay the night. In the morning he proceeded on his way, but he had not gone far when he noticed that his horse had become lame. Arriving at a blacksmiths he asked the owner to look at the horse. The smithy found some wire between the shoe and the foot and told the traveller it must have been deliberately put there. The traveller said he was not afraid of anyone, as he had a brace of pistols with which to defend himself. But on examination it was found that the gunpowder had been removed and substituted with bran. The pistols were then correctly loaded and the horseman continued on his way. He had not gone far along the narrow, lonely lane, when he was stopped at Ringley Oak by a man in disguise. The traveller immediately fired his pistols and in the words of the story, 'the landlord of the White Lion, one Filewood, dropped dead'.

It would be fair to comment that Mr Filewood was an exceptionally "Rogue Landlord", as the White Lion has enjoyed a high reputation for hospitality over many centuries. Certainly by 1790 it was a much respected focal point of Linkfield Sreet and the accepted meeting -place for the local inhabitants. Though it had not grown significantly over the years, Linkfield Street had historic connections and was important enough to be marked on successive maps of Reigate Hundred. Like the other pocket communities, it had grown around the Manor of Linkfield which had been first mentioned in 1315, when it was owned by Nicholas de Lynkefeld. The manor house stood on what used to be the corner of Station Road and Linkfield Lane, before the roundabout was built. By the end of the seventeen hundreds, ownership had passed to the Ladbroke family, who also possessed the Frenches estate. But its days as a family residence were also numbered and though it was used as a hospital for survivors of the Walcheren expedition in 1809, it fell into disrepair and was demolished towards the middle of the century.

But by the end of the eighteenth century the general administration of Linkfield Street was no longer the concern of the Ladbrokes. For as a recognised hamlet the people elected their own constable and surveyor, as well as keeping their roads in reasonable repair. They were a close-knit community and a caring one too, ensuring that the well and pump opposite the White Lion was kept in working order. Not that it was used much by the local inhabitants, as most had their own wells, a fact which was substantiated many years later when various remains were found in the gardens of houses in Charman and Fengates roads. But the community well was welcomed by travellers as was the bowling green near the old High Trees farm, which was used by customers who stayed at the inn.

Though the White Lion may have been regarded as the focal point for social life, the tannery was most definitely the centre of business. By 1800 it was firmly established, having enjoyed continuous trading since the Blatt family owned it one hundred years earlier. It was also ideally situated along the lower end of Linkfield Street and across the area of what is now Tannery Close. Perhaps considered modest in size and output if compared with today's massive business houses, the tannery was undoubtedly an important influence in the early commercial life of the district. A fact for which a series of owners must take credit, as their successors would have done in continuing the business into the second half of the twentieth century. Though the tannery expanded considerably in these later years, it was of sufficient importance in 1800 for its owner John Wright to report that it comprised;

"a dwelling house, barn, stable, kiln, bark mill,
tanyard, out-buildings, garden, orchard and two
acres of meadow".

Certainly the tannery was a continuing success story for John Wright and his employees, as Linkfield Street and the rest of Reigate Foreign prepared to greet the new century. A new century which in a few short years would witness dramatic changes; changes which were already in progress outside this rural community; changes which the gathering momentum of the industrial revolution were bringing ever closer.

THE RIGHT HON. LORD MONSON.

Dr Clair Grece, Town Clerk of Reigate from January 1864 until his death in December 1905

"From an early hour in the morning the streets presented a scene of the utmost activity. Every train brought a large number of visitors to the town, and soon the streets were crowded with spectators, who, to their credit be it said, behaved in the most orderly manner. Every available spot from which a view of the arrival of the distinguished company could be obtained was occupied by spectators. At three o'clock the special train conveying the Royal party stopped at the temporary siding erected near the schools. Here fitting preparations had been made, under the management of Mr. W. Nash, the stationmaster, for the reception of the Prince and Princess, who were accompanied by three of the Princesses. Their Royal Highnesses were attended by Lord and Lady Suffield, Lieut.-General Sir Dighton Probyn, and Colonel Arthur Ellis. A guard of honour was furnished by the 2nd Volunteer Battalion of the Queen's (Royal West Surrey) Regiment.

"On alighting from the saloon carriage in which they had travelled, the party was received by the Mayor (R. Field, Esq.) and the members of the Corporation of Reigate, also by the President (the Archbishop of Canterbury), and the members of the committee and officers of the Royal Asylum of St. Anne's.

"The daughter of Mr. John Shaw, J.P., of Buckhurst, presented the Princess, on her arrival, with a bouquet ; one of the smallest children of the St. Anne's Society also presented the Princess with a bouquet.

"The Mayor presented the following address of welcome:—

"'TO THEIR ROYAL HIGHNESSES THE PRINCE AND PRINCESS OF
"'WALES.

"'May it please your Royal Highnesses,

"'We, the Mayor, Aldermen, and Burgesses of the Borough of Reigate, desire the honour of being permitted, after the lapse of fifteen years, to renew the expression of our unswerving attachment to your Royal Highnesses, and to the person and family of Her Majesty the Queen.

"'When, upon a former occasion, your Royal Highnesses deigned to tarry for a brief space of time within the confines of this municipality, it was to countenance, by your gracious presence, at a ceremony similar to that which is to be performed to-day, the enlargement and extension of a benevolent establishment—the Earlswood Asylum. The character for salubrity, now so well and widely known, enjoyed by our borough, has since attracted within our borders another institution, the Schools of the Royal Asylums of St. Anne, which, however different in the objects which it is destined to benefit, has its source in the same sympathy for the less fortunate members of the human family.

"'Nothing doubting that the visit of your Royal Highnesses will stimulate yet further the spirit of charity and beneficence among the wealthy and prosperous of our land, we beg to be allowed to tender to your Royal Highnesses our most loyal and respectful thanks for the honour conferred upon us and our borough, and for the encouragement which, by this your gracious visit, you have been pleased to afford to the Royal Asylum of St. Anne's Society.

"' Given under our common seal, this 9th day of July, 1884.

"' By order of the Council,

"'ROBERT FIELD, Mayor.

"'CLAIR J. GRECE, LL.D., Town Clerk.'

" The Prince replied as follows :—

"' Mr. Mayor and Gentlemen,—I beg to thank you on behalf of the Princess of Wales, as well as on my own, for your cordial address of welcome on the occasion of this our second visit to Reigate. I rejoice to perceive that, during the fifteen years which have elapsed since we were last here, great improvements have been effected in your borough and its neighbourhood, and that the inhabitants have not neglected to avail themselves of the excellent opportunities which are afforded to them by the salubrious climate and advantages of the situation of your town. These conditions render Reigate peculiarly suitable as a site for such institutions as this school, whose enlargement and improvement we are assembled to commemorate to-day. It has always been our endeavour to encourage by our presence the formation and extension of charitable works throughout the kingdom, and we thank you for the kind words in which you show your appreciation of our exertions.' (Cheers.)

"Their Royal Highnesses were then conducted to the Royal Pavilion by the Lord Lieutenant (Earl Lovelace), the High Sheriff of the County (John Henderson, Esq., of Leatherhead), and the President and Members of the Committee of the Society. Among those present were :—The High Sheriff of Surrey, Earl and Countess Lovelace, Lord and Lady Monson, Sir E. and Lady Watkin, Hon. and Rev. Canon Legge, Col. and the Hon. Mrs. Armytage, Sir S. and Lady Waterlow, General Sir R. Wilbraham, Sir Trevor Lawrence, M.P., Sir W. G. Anderson, Sir Valentine Fleming, Sir G. Macleay, Mr. W. Grantham, Q.C., M.P., Col. and Mrs. Paine, Lady Henry Somerset, Col. Searle, Mr. and Mrs. Beaumont, the Mayor of Croydon and Lady, the Archdeacon of Surrey and Lady, the Mayor of Guildford, Mr. Sheriff Cowan, the Master of the Cordwainers' Company, Mr., Mrs., and Miss Waterlow, the Master of the Vintners' Company, Mr. Sheriff Smith and Lady, Mr. Alderman and Mrs. Gray, the Master of the Salters' Company, Mr. H. Edwards, M.P., Mr. J. Shaw, J.P.

" Sir H. W. Peek, Bart., was prevented from being present by the lamented death of Lady Peek, but with his usual beneficence promised the handsome donation of 250 guineas.

" The band of the Scots Guards performed.

" The daïs was erected under a large and handsome marquee. The royal ladies remained standing till the advent of the Prince, who had meanwhile met the principal officers of the Grand Lodge of England. The Provincial Grand Lodge of Surrey had been opened in this new building at three o'clock.

"' Presently the Prince, attended by his Grand Officers, proceeded from the Royal Pavilion to the site in the following order :—

Assistant Grand Pursuivant.
Grand Pursuivant.
Grand Organist.
Assistant Grand Director of Ceremonies.
Deputy Grand Director of Ceremonies.
Grand Director of Ceremonies (Sir Albert Woods).
Three Grand Officers, bearing the Cornucopia, and ewers with wine and oil.
Grand Superintendent of Works, bearing a Plate with the Inscription
for the Foundation Stone.
Grand Secretary for German Correspondence.
Grand Secretary, carrying the Trowel.
President of the Board of General Purposes, carrying the Mallet.
Grand Registrar.
Grand Treasurer (Colonel Creaton), bearing a Phial containing the Coins to
be deposited in the Stone.
The Junior Grand Warden (Lord Mayor Fowler, M.P.), with the Plumb
Rule.
The City Architect (Mr. Horace Jones).
The Senior Grand Warden (Lord Cremorne), with the Level.
Junior Grand Deacon (Mr. Leitchworth).
The Grand Chaplains.
The Deputy Grand Master of England (the Earl of Lathom), with the
Square.
The Prov. Grand Master of Norfolk (Lord Suffield).
Grand Secretary (Colonel Shadwell Clarke).
Grand Standard Bearers, carrying their Banners.
The Grand Sword Bearer, carrying the Sword.
The Most Worshipful the Grand Master (The Prince of Wales, K.G.).
Senior Grand Deacon (Baron de Ferrières).
Grand Tyler.

"On arrival at the entrance his Royal Highness was received by the Committee of the Society and conducted to the daïs. The scene in the marquee was now most brilliant and impressive. The Grand Master and the Brethren adorned with their costly insignia, the various other dignitaries with their robes, the well-dressed throng of spectators, the coloured hangings, the luxuriously appointed daïs—all illuminated at the moment by the brilliant sunshine—made up a picture of greatest interest, and which will not soon be forgotten by any who were present. The 'Hymn of Praise' was first sung by the children of the Asylum, afterwards the Lord Bishop of Rochester offered up an appropriate prayer.

"The President of the Society (the Archbishop) then addressed the Grand Master, and requested him to lay the stone. He said: This Society, called the St. Anne's Society, of which I have the honour to be President, has almost completed the second century of its existence. It was founded in the year 1702, when a great many noble institutions were founded by the same great men who presided over the ancient Society for the Propagation of the Gospel in Foreign Parts. The object of this Society is to receive, to help, clothe, and educate the children who it is agreed are the poorest of all, whether orphans or no—who, having been born in a superior position, find themselves almost destitute. It is also a remarkable feature in this Society that it receives the children of any nation, and in that it is particularly endued with the English characteristic of hospitality. It has received up to this time and provided for almost 4,000 children. It has no endowment whatever, but entirely depends upon the voluntary contributions of the public. Its removal to this place has been necessitated by the Society's children outgrowing their present home at Streatham, and it is now intended by the founding of these new schools to provide at least for four hundred children. This occasion, upon which your Royal Highness has graciously condescended to be present to lay the foundation or memorial stone, is one of immense interest to the place.

"The Prince was then conducted to the stone, which hung suspended from a tripod, and over a lower stone, immediately in front of the daïs, and took up his position, and the vessels of coin, wine, and oil were deposited on a pedestal placed for their reception. The upper stone was raised and the lower one adjusted.

"The Prince of Wales then addressed the assembly, and, prayer having been offered by the Grand Chaplain, the Grand Secretary read the following inscription on the plate:—'This corner stone of the Chapel of the Royal Asylum of St. Anne's Society was laid by H.R.H. Albert Edward Prince of Wales, K.G., &c., Worshipful Grand Master of Freemasons, on the 9th July, 1884.'

"The Grand Treasurer then deposited the phial containing the coins, and the Grand Secretary placed the plate on the lower stone. The cement was then spread on the upper face of the lower stone, and the M.W. the Grand Master adjusted the same with a trowel handed to him for the purpose, after which the upper stone was slowly lowered with three distinct stops. The cornucopia containing the corn, and the ewers with the wine and oil, were next handed to him, and the Grand Master strewed the corn and poured the wine and oil over the stone with the accustomed ceremonies. The architect was presented to the Grand Master, and delivered to His Royal Highness the plan of the intended building.

"Purses were presented by a large number of ladies and children, and the sum reached a total of £3,000.

"This ceremony having been completed, the Mayor (R. Field, Esq.) addressing His Royal Highness, said: 'May it please your Royal Highness, the members of the Council of the Royal Asylum of St. Anne's Society are most unwilling that this great event should pass away without some record of your Royal Highness's great kindness in coming to serve the Society in the manner in which you have done to-day. The Society desires that your Royal Highness will be graciously pleased to accept a presentation from the Society. If your Royal Highness will do that, you will confer a lasting favour on the Society.' (Cheers.)

"The Prince of Wales briefly thanked the Mayor, and, the blessing having been pronounced by the Archbishop, the Royal party left the building. The Prince at once drove, in company with the Princess and the three Princesses, through the principal streets of the town to the residence of Mr. W. B. Waterlow, J.P., High Trees. The Earl of Lovelace, Lord Monson, Mr. Waterlow, the Mayor, and several other distinguished persons followed in separate carriages. The route was lined with spectators, who heartily cheered the distinguished visitors as they passed through the town. The demonstration on their return to Redhill Junction, where a special train was in waiting to convey them to London, was no less hearty and enthusiastic."

Chapter 3
THE RAILWAYMEN COMETH

Though the effects of the Industrial Revolution, which were sweeping other parts of the country, were not to reach rural Reigate Foreign for some years, plans were already being drawn up to improve transport communications in the south of England. It was generally accepted that the main coaching roads were no longer able to cope with the increase in commercial traffic. Other methods were needed and needed urgently, to transport the products of the industrial north to the continent as well as the south of England. Canals had proved most effective in the north and other parts of the country and, apart from construction costs, were economical to maintain and run. But when the engineer John Rennie proposed a canal to Portsmouth via Croydon and Redhill, with a four and a half mile tunnel north of Merstham, the plans were rejected.

Meanwhile, as the talking continued, action had already been taken with the launch of the Surrey Iron Railway. Initially it ran from a wharf at the mouth of the River Wandle at Wandsworth, through Earlsfield, across Mitcham Common via Carshalton, to a terminus in a field on the site of West Croydon Station. The line was then extended from the terminus to Merstham and Godstone but the railway was never used as a passenger service. The wagons were pulled by horses and regularly carried lime from Quarry Dean, which now lies disused near the M23 on a track that leads to Limeworks Road just north of Merstham. It quickly proved a popular way of transporting other bulk freight including, chalk, Fullers Earth, timber and firestone. Apart from these, the company's Notice of Tolls in 1804 drew the public's attention to another commodity.

"FOR DUNG --per ton, per mile, - 1d."

For a time there was general disbelief that horses were capable of pulling heavy wagons loaded with firestone and lime. In order to quash these rumours a demonstration was arranged and the public invited to attend.

"On this occasion a number of gentlemen assembled near Merstham to see this extraordinary 'triumph of art'. For a wager twelve wagons were loaded with firestones, each wagon weighing over three tons. These were chained together and a horse, taken from a timber cart, was yoked to the chain of wagons and started from the Fox Public House to draw this immense load (36 tons) right into Croydon, six miles away. The horse did the journey at the rate of four miles an hour. The horse was stopped dead four times to show that it was not by impetus that the power was acquired. Having won the wager four more wagons were added to this train and loaded with fifty workmen. Still the horse pulled this added weight along without distress. After this trial the whole of the filled wagons were weighed. They scaled 55 tons''.

Though the railway enjoyed a relatively short existence, its services were extensively used by one local company and were largely responsible for establishing another. By 1839 around 6000 tons of Fullers Earth were being transported annually from the Nutfield and Redhill pits. And a good deal of this was taken in bags on a specially constructed tramtrack, to the Iron Railway at Merstham and from there to London. Some years earlier in 1824, George Hall had taken a lease on the quarries at Merstham and, because of the help he received from the railway, was able to form a small family business. By 1898 this small family business had grown large enough to be incorporated, with the result that today Hall & Company is one of the principal trading firms of its type in Redhill and the South East. But 1839 was to be the last year for the Surrey Iron Railway, as with growing financial problems and an antiquated rail system, it was forced to sell its land to the fledgeling London, Brighton and South Coast Railway.

Though the Iron Railway was a boon for the traders, the plight of the general public remained. However, an improvement was made in 1808 with the opening of a new London to Brighton road, through Croydon and Merstham to Reigate. But the easier less hilly extension from Gatton through Redhill to Povey Cross was deferred, despite representations by the Prince Regent that he disliked the hills of Reigate. Later to become George IV, he was a frequent traveller from London to Brighton to ''savour the air''. While it can be assumed that the Prince Regent was influential in ''speeding up'' the process of extending the road through Redhill, the needs of the growing population had also to be considered. In fact by 1801 Reigate Foreign had outgrown Reigate and there were now 221 houses and over 1300 inhabitants. But in Reigate there remained stiff opposition to any new road which would divert trade from the town. And this opposition from the traders had the weighty backing of Lord Somers, through whose lands the proposed road would have to be constructed.

Arguments continued inside and outside Parliament for some years, but eventually in 1816 an Act was passed permitting the road to be built. The original plan was for it to pass through the uninhabited marshland of Redhill and follow the brook to the site of the future Royal Earlswood Hospital, since this would have been the less hilly option. But the forceful objections of Lord Somers and the Reigate Turnpike Trust prevailed, resulting in the construction of the present road. This was also Lord Somers' land, but he no doubt felt that the hill would be a deterrent for stage-coaches. This assumption turned out to be wrong and because it was a more direct route to the coast, the road was immediately popular, though there were problems in wet weather. Coaches and other horse-drawn vehicles had no brakes and had to rely on "skid pans", which were wooden or metal devices used to prevent the wheels turning. This usually involved work for an extra man and one of Earlswood's early residents was soon on the scene. He went by the name of Brown and operated from the crown of the hill approximately where The Cutting is now. At this point he would climb on a coach and skid the wheels down the hill for a few coppers, returning back to his post by the next transport.

The line of the road south to Horley is thought to be close to a north to south track, which existed in the Neolithic Age. This theory is based on the discovery of an old axehead just south of Salfords, which itself dates from Saxon times and literally means, "ford by the willows". By 1300 a lane existed through the village and crossed over Mason's Brook by means of a wooden bridge. From Salfords the lane crossed Petridgewood Common to Woodhatch, where it joined up with the main road from Reigate. Prior to the nineteenth century it was used only for local traffic and, as such, little attention was given to its condition. In fact in the winter it was usually a quagmire of mud and virtually impassable.

In the fifteenth century the authorities endeavoured to persuade local inhabitants to assist with maintenance but without much success. There appeared to be general apathy and, in some instances, wilful destruction of public property. This was mainly directed at wooden bridges and in particular the one at Salfords which,

> "is in great decay and the borough of Woodlatch and the Borough of Earbridge ought to make new the way".

Whether improvements were made is not recorded but one of the culprits, John Shoe, was caught and fine 8d;

> "for conveying various rails, fences and footrails from Mason's Bridge and converting them to his own use, being to the prejudice of all the inhabitants of Northborough, and a bad example to all the people".

With the opening of the road through the Redhill area to join the lane just north of Salfords, conditions improved. But it was some years later, with the introduction of tarmacadam, before the surface could be called "good in all weathers". The erection of turnpike gates and toll-houses north of Redhill and at Salfords meant that travellers had to pay for their passage. If tolls were refused collectors were authorised to seize any horse, "together with bridle and saddle, or any carriage along with its goods". The tolls were fixed by Act of Parliament and varied according to the type of "carriage" using the road. Farmers driving animals were also charged, although foot-travellers appear to have been allowed to pass freely.

> "For every Horse or other Beast of Draught drawing any Coach, Sociable, Berlin, Landau, Chariot, Vis a Vis, Chaise, Calash, Chaise Marine, Curricle, Chair, Gig, Whiskey, Caravan, Hearse, Litter or other such carriage, the sum of fourpence.
> For every Horse...drawing any Waggon, Cart or Dray having the bottom of the Fellies of the Wheels...nine inches or upwards, threepence".

With the opening of this more direct route to Brighton, traffic increased and brought new business to the area. But the original reason for the new road was not that travellers might reach their destinations quicker, but that it would "....render the intercourse between the Metropolis and Sea Coast more speedy, particularly in the supply of fish in the Mackerel and Herring Season".

One of the first recipients of this new business was ironically Lord Somers, or more accurately his relative James Cocks, to whom he granted a piece of common land at the corner of Mill Street. With an eye for business,

Cocks immediately built an inn and posting house for his benefit and the needs of the increasing numbers of travellers. Grateful to his uncle he called it The Somers Arms, but its life as an inn was short-lived with the subsequent arrival of the railways and the decrease in stage-coach traffic. But at least for some years it was a regular stopping-place for travellers, "who would dine and drink at the inn, or perhaps climb Red Hill Common by a footpath at the back, while they waited for the coach to continue". Designed in the Regency style with two distinctive bow windows, the house later became St. John's Church vicarage. Today The Firs still retains some of its Regency grandeur in the original part adjacent to the traffic lights.

However, there were other beneficiaries of the new "business boom" in Mill Street, which at the time was referred to as the "chief town in the Manor of Hooley". A somewhat grand description for a mere hamlet consisting of a dozen cottages, a pub and a blacksmith. Though now crossed by the new Brighton Road, Mill Street extended as far as the old watermill past the Marquis of Granby and was assuming some importance. In fact a reference to the pub in 1827 confirmed that there were,

> "close by it three more houses and the new inn, the Somers Arms, kept by Mr Relf".

Meanwhile at Gatton the progress of modern developments had done nothing to change the Rotten Borough system. Despite the fact that the area was still sparsely populated and only the landed gentry permitted to vote, the Borough continued to return two members to Westminster. But hope was "around the corner" and in 1832 the Reform Act changed this unjust system, largely due to the unrelenting efforts of William Cobbett of RURAL RIDES fame. All his life he had been an advocate of bettering the working man's lot. In particular he wanted parliamentary reform and published a newspaper in which he aired his views. THE POLITICAL REGISTER sold over two hundred thousand copies and was immensely popular. For his sins he "did time" in Newgate Prison, but this did not deter his efforts and he continued to uphold the democratic rights of the working classes. However, Lord Monson, the new owner of Gatton, was far from happy with the Act since, having paid a considerable sum of money for the property, he no longer had any political power.

The dissolution of the old Rotten Boroughs system of electing members of Parliament, prompted William Bryant to "have a go" at the local gentry and in particular the Somers family. He was involved in local administration and quite outspoken for his generation.

"For upwards of 100 years Reygate has been more than rotten, if possible, than the Borough of Gatton....and for the great part of that period usurped by the family of Cocks(Somers),"

Taking the opportunity to criticise the Somers family for objecting to the original proposed route of the Brighton Road, he observed;

"....Let us now examine what has been the conduct of the now Lord Somers and his father, to the inhabitants of Reygate. First the two great inns in the town were permitted to be occupied by one man, whence the travellers on the Brighton Road complained of the grossest extortions and want of accomodations. The public not choosing to submit to this, projected a new road, to avoid Reygate town altogether; and Howleigh Park, formerly my estate, was cut through the centre, to make the same, (whereby a loss occurred to myself and the gentleman with whom I exchanged it of upwards of £2000), instead of its going by Howleigh House in the bottom (by the Brook), where it ought to have gone....but by this job, the public were obliged to pass a hill where a house called the Somers Arms has been erected. ....and the public having a hill to pass both ways; when the road by going in the other direction would have had no hill at all".

But this in-fighting between the gentry, which continued unabated throughout the eighteen thirties, was of little concern to the working people. Nor were they too worried that these gentlemen were no longer able to shoot snipe and other game in the marshlands beside the Brighton Road. In fact the road provided new opportunities for work in the boggy wastes, where stray cattle often sank to their loins and had to be pulled out with ropes. Though this was only occasional work for the unemployed, many of them were soon fully engaged with the upkeep of the road itself. Digging stones from the Common was not easy work, but it meant money and full stomachs. Today, some of the pits and trenches can be seen but most are now covered in vegetation.

Though the increase in the population was still only gradual, the mill at

Blackborough found it necessary to take on more workers to meet the demands. And so did the new mill on Wray Common which had been built in 1824. Situated nearer Reigate it also served the Redhill area, where in later years the Cooke family opened a bakery in Station Road. The Blackborough area was still rural, but by the eighteen thirties a number of dwellings had been built along the road to Reigate. Amongst them was the business of Simeon Shaw, blacksmith and wheelwright, who bought the land originally belonging to the old workhouse. When he retired his son William continued the business for a while but, sensing another important need, turned the building into an ale house. The property was later bought by a brewery and enlarged but still retained parts of the smithy. Because of its prime position The Forester's Arms attracted passing trade, which it continues to do today under the more traditional name of The Hatch.

But none of these rural happenings compared with the heated debates that were raging in Parliament over the proposed railway linking London with Brighton. Even the furore caused by the building of the Brighton Road paled in comparison. For between 1833 and 1837, no fewer than six routes had been proposed, each prepared by a different engineer and, as a consequence, creating a considerable amount of animosity. In 1841 the London and Brighton Railway Guide noted that;

"In 1835, a year prolific in railway schemes, no fewer than four lines between London and Brighton were projected, brought before and supported by the public. And in 1836 a contest of as keen a character as was ever known in Parliament for a private Bill, was carried on between the supporters of the competing lines each striving for the mastery. During the Parliament contest, London was in a state of ferment on the subject. In 1837 the contest recommenced with renewed vigour and fury, but Parliament, weary and utterly sick of the question, placed it in the hands of a Commissioner to decide on the merits of the respective lines. His report was in favour of the Direct Line which was immediately sanctioned by the Legislature".

This decision obviously delighted the successful engineer Sir John Rennie and his employers The London, Brighton and South Coast Railway, who immediately became incorporated and began work. Meanwhile the South

Eastern Railway's proposals for a route to Dover, had been the subject of long debate and several changes. The obvious direct route via Maidstone or Gravesend and Canterbury came to nothing, as did their original proposal for a line across the Weald, which would have passed several miles east of Redhill, through Croydon and Godstone. By the time the Company received Parliamentary approval in June 1836, this plan had been amended for the line to run even further east through Riddlesdown and Oxted. Work had already started on Riddlesdown tunnel when, a year later, the passing of the London and Brighton Railway Act provided the South Eastern with the cost-saving alternative of extending its line westwards to join the Brighton line at Redhill.

During the next few years the untouched countryside of southern England underwent dramatic transformation, as tunnels were driven through hills, bridges built and hundreds of miles of tracks laid across virgin fields. At Merstham thousands of workers were brought in from the Midlands, Yorkshire and Ireland, to dig out the tunnel. While further south more were employed constructing the embankment across the marshlands from Wiggey to Salfords. This work was made relatively easy by using the soil from the cuttings north and south of the Merstham tunnel and from the tunnel itself. But it was inevitable that with a mixed workforce, trouble would soon break out between the different factions. This usually happened on pay days as drunken navvies roamed around swearing and fighting. Even closing the doors of public houses had little effect as they were able to obtain liquor from other sources. Their behaviour obviously caused considerable consternation amongst the local inhabitants, for they were described on more than one occasion as, "the most uncultivated beings on earth" Unfortunately the fights also broke out at work and it was rumoured that in one of "these affairs", a navvy was killed and his body buried in the embankment near the Three Arches. However, this was not the only trouble the local community had on their hands, but some of their number may have been responsible for it. For it was now apparent that the stage-coaches would quickly become obsolete, as trains were a good deal faster if not necessarily more comfortable. Whether the coach proprietors themselves were actually responsible is debatable, but gangs of thugs were hired to create as much trouble as possible on the railways. As a result fights were frequent and many became riots.

The original plan was to have a station at Reigate but the authorities refused to have one in or anywhere near it. Having had enough opposition in getting the railway approved in the first place, the London and Brighton opted for a station at Battlebridge and another to the south at Hooley Lane, to be called Red Hill and Reigate Road. At the same time the South Eastern had commenced work on their line eastwards to Tonbridge and they, too, thought Hooley Lane was an ideal site for a station. In 1841 a service on the London to Brighton line was started and a year later the South Eastern began operating trains to Tonbridge. But when the South Eastern decided to change the name of their station in Hooley Lane from Redstone Hill to Reigate, there was understandably considerable confusion. But from the start neither railway company had any intention of co-operating with each other, And it was a saga of acrimonious discord that was destined to continue for years, with the public the unhappy victims.

Having adjusted to the confusion of having two "Reigate" stations within a few hundred yards of one another, passengers were now faced with the problems of changing trains. Though the distance between the two stations was not great, no thought at all had been given to improving Hooley Lane, despite the mounting complaints from passengers. And they had good cause to complain as the road remained muddy, narrow and ill-lit and at one point crossed the brook over an antiquated and highly dangerous bridge. But since the Reigate authorities had not wanted the railways this was not surprising, even though Hooley Lane was still the principal east to west highway. But though it was close to the houses and the two stations, it was still unsafe for others travelling by coach or chaise. Mrs Grece, whose husband was the last High Constable of Reigate Hundred, kept a diary which makes interesting reading. She was an observant lady and spent much time in the Redhill district travelling around.

> "Feb 1st 1837 - Coming back with the horse a little before ten, we were frightened at the bottom of Redstone Hill by some tramps. We heard a low whistle, which we did not like, so(we) made the horse go pretty fast and we got home all right.
> "March 19th - On our return from a walk met at the Brook five men who were looking about the intended railroad.

> "April 15th - Before dinner to see a stag turned out in Earlswood.
>
> "June 4th 1840 - We walked to Red Hill to see the steam coach.
>
> "May 21st 1841 - We had a pleasant walk to Horley on the rails. Near to our journey's end we met with Mr Rastrick (Railway Superintendent) and were told by him we must discontinue the practice of walking on the line.
>
> "July 12th - The Brighton Railway opened to the public for the first time. We went to Red Hill to see two trains.
>
> "July 16th - A man was killed near Horley last evening on the Brighton Line. His own fault. He was in liquor and he attempted to leave the engine while it was going. He fell and spoke no more."

But this was not the only accident to occur that year, for shortly before the railway was extended to Brighton in September, a train ran into a line of horse-drawn wagons near Hooley and was derailed. This incident was not recorded by Mrs Grece, though her son Dr C.J. Grece who was then a young man, recalled these early days of the railway many years later.

"The first railway line was that to Brighton, opened in 1841. I well remember it being built during the two previous years, notably that a locomotive was employed in conveying the soil from the Merstham tunnel to form the embankment where the Junction (Redhill Station) now stands; also the embankment across Earlswood Common. Here the works were over and over again suspended for slips. A slippery clay was used, which widened out laterally like so much sludge. I may here relate that the only road east and west ran down Redstone Hollow and in front of the house at Hooley occupied formerly by Lady Mostyn, later by Mr Rennie, and thence over Whitepost Hill. The railway crossed the road near the brook obliquely, and the archway should have been built askew, but the engineer or contractor, to save bricks, built it at right angles, with the result that the pillars of the arch encroached some eighteen inches upon the highway in two places. The road surveyors were aroused, when the bridge was nearly completed, to this encroachment, and demanded the demolition of the bridge. The railway people remonstrated upon the hardship of this, whereby the construction of the railway would have been greatly retarded, seeing that the soil had to be conveyed over it for building the line further on. The public was inexorable, and having the company in its power, imposed upon it, as the condition of the bridge's being suffered to remain, that the company should at its own cost, lower Whitepost Hill 12 feet, and also make a new straight section of road eastward of the railway, with a bridge in substitution for the ancient curved line of road with the ford through the brook. This must have been a very costly bargain for the company, many times more than it would have cost to build an askew bridge at first, but the company having to submit either to this expense or to a great delay in the construction of the line, chose the former. Let me say however, that the former line of the road, with the footbridge only over the brook and which ran in front of the houses, although abandoned by the public, and now taken into the plantations, has never been legally closed. A right of public carriageway still exists along the ancient line.

  The station was where the Brighton goods station now is (Hockley Estate). The line was opened on the 28th June 1841, at first as far as Haywards Heath only. This is recorded in my mother's journal thus; 'Steam carriages to Haywards Heath today. They appeared to go nicely. They passed here between 12 and 1 o'clock and returned in the afternoon'. The line was opened the whole way to Brighton on Tuesday 21st September, after which the trains became more numerous than the one up and one down each day".

  For a period in the early years, the only people who travelled by rail were the wealthy. Then the second class was introduced so that servants and lesser mortals, need not share the same carriages as their "betters". The introduction of a third class some years later, left much to be desired, though the labouring folk who travelled in them were a hardy breed and well used to the elements. And indeed they needed to be, for the carriages which they and "others of mean circumstances" travelled in, were little more than open cattle trucks with wooden benches. Railway Officials would not even allow a passenger to take a bag into the carriage, in case it was used as a seat and by doing so, "he obtained more comfort than the fare of one penny a mile allowed".

As Dr Grece remarked;

> "These carriages were open to the sky, and the seats were of lathes, that the rain might pass through. The rain and snow, and the ashes from the engine, pelted in the faces of the passengers who faced the engine".

These conditions prevailed until laws were passed in 1854 forcing railway companies to provide covered wagons, but even then they only had wooden slats over windows instead of glass. In the meantime the long-suffering passengers had to put up with further inconveniences, when the South Eastern decided to move their station. It was another example of the disdain both companies had for each other. But the occasion was momentous, as it followed the final connection of the South Eastern's line to Dover on 7th February 1844, when the first train pulled out of London Bridge station bound for Dover. It was pulled by the locomotive "Shakespeare" and among the passengers were members of the South Eastern Railway Board. The arrival of the train at Dover several hours later was greeted with a gun salute from Archcliffe Fort and a dinner organised by the town corporation.

Though passengers may not have considered the event momentous at the time, the opening of the new station on 15th April was effectively the first stage in the birth of Redhill town. Indeed few of them, if any, could possibly have foreseen a town being built in the boglands that surrounded the station. For them it was isolated, ill-chosen and inhospitable; a clutter of iron girders that afforded no relief from the icy blasts that swept south from the Downs. No place to linger; no place to call home...at least not yet.

Redhill Common 1845 Looking N.W over Shaw's Corner
(courtesy Redhill Library)

The railway junctions at Redhill in the late 1840s. The main SER line is in the foreground with the Brighton line in the middle. (courtesy Redhill Library)

OLD BAPTIST CHAPEL, STATION ROAD, REDHILL.

A South Eastern Railway engine of the 1850's

The business of John Moody, wheelwright which he founded in 1830. In the 1950s the business was being run as a garage by G.F. Graves & Son, whose proprietor George was the great grandson of John Moody. The site at 113 Brighton Road is now occupied by Baker Redhill.
(courtesy Redhill Library)

W. SANDERS & SON,

FAMILY GROCERS, TEA-DEALERS,

PROVISION MERCHANTS,

AND

ITALIAN WAREHOUSEMEN,

WARWICK HOUSE,

RED HILL.

SUPERIOR BRITISH WINES.

Agent for Huntley & Palmer's celebrated Reading Biscuits—Daries of Fresh Butter Daily—Fine York Hams and Wiltshire Bacon—Stilton, Cheshire, Cheddar and Other Cheese.

Families waited on for orders.

T. CLIFTON,

WARWICK BREWERY, STATION ROAD RED HILL,

Pale Ale and Porter Brewer.

FAMILIES SUPPLIED WITH ALL KINDS OF PALE ALES AND PORTER AT THE FOLLOWING PRICES :—

BITTER ALE.

Light Table Ale in Casks of 4½—9 and 18-gallons	at	1/ per gal.
Pale Bitter Ale in ditto	at	1/2 ,,

MILD ALES.

X Ale in Casks of 4½—9 and 18-gallons	at	/7 ,,
XX Ale in ditto ditto	at	1/ ,,
XXX Ale in ditto ditto	at	1/6 ,,

PORTER.

Porter in Casks of 4½—9 and 18-gallons	at	1/2 ,,
Double Stout	at	1/6 ,,
TrebleTable Extra Stout	at	1/8 ,,

ALL ORDERS BY POST PUNCTUALLY ATTENDED TO.

Edward Lambert, the tradesman Mayor in 1878

Advertisements.

The SURREY MIRROR,

Reigate and Redhill Reporter,

AND GENERAL COUNTY ADVERTISER.

COUNTY NEWSPAPER,

Published Friday Evening, for Saturday, 1d. Weekly,

56 COLUMNS.

QUARTERLY SUBSCRIPTION, POST FREE, 1s. 8d.

Resident Reporters in the following Towns:—

Reigate,   Croydon,   Guildford,
Godalming,   Caterham,   Dorking,
Horsham,   Godstone,   Crawley.

The Surrey Mirror
Is the Best Medium for Advertising
IN THE COUNTY OF SURREY.

☞ *The Surrey Mirror* ☜

Is an Old-Established Journal, and Circulates not only in SURREY, but KENT and SUSSEX.

CHIEF OFFICES:—

REDHILL, SURREY.

Chapter 4
WARWICK TOWN

The construction of the railways was not the only event taking place in those early years of Queen Victoria's reign. Perhaps it went unnoticed by the thousands of workers digging out the tunnel at Merstham and shifting the great quantities of earth to form the embankments. But when some of these very workers were laid off and they made their homes in 'shanty' type huts at St. Johns, the name Little London took on a new significance. For their arrival had an immediate impact and by 1840 the population in the area of Red Hill, Linkfield Street and Woodhatch had reached 1200. The decision to build St. John's Church was taken in 1840 at a public meeting, when a proposal made by Sir W.G.H. Joliffe was seconded and carried unanimously.

> "I therefore now move that this meeting, being well aware that the Mother Church of the Parish of Reigate is incapable of affording church room for its increasing population and that consequently a large portion of the Parish is from the very circumstances of the case deprived of the benefit resulting from the ministrations of the Church of England, do now call upon the friends of that church strenuously to exert themselves to provide a remedy for the evil which they so feelingly deplore".

In 1841 it was decided to build on a site to be carved out of common land on a "knoll of rising ground, midway down a hillside" and known as Knobb's Hill. The good Lord Somers generously granted the lease and work began almost immediately. Known at first as the Redhill District Church, it was consecrated by the Bishop of Winchester on 30th September 1843. The following year it became the fully-fledged ecclesiastical parish of St. John the Evangelist, but it was not until 1895 after radical alterations that the tower and spire with eight bells were added.

The clearance of the squatters' huts from Knobb's Hill, or Flint's Hill as it was sometimes referred to, was widely welcomed and resulted in a number of new cottages being built in and around the Plough Inn. St. Johns was an ideal village setting and one which must have attracted William Verrall to make his home there. Born in 1763, he arrived from Sussex towards the end of that century and moved into one of the cottages on The Knobb, which he held copyhold from the Manor of Reigate. The Knobb, as distinct from Knobb's Hill, is the area of land in Common Road stretching from the Albatross pub to the railway embankment. And this probably accounts for the old Railway Inn becoming known by the same name. But in 1800 there was no Common Road or inn; just a couple of old farm cottages and a house which belonged to a Mr Hollis. No railway line either, that in later years was to take away a major portion of the Verrall orchard. In 1802, having by now settled down comfortably, William Verrall purchased from Lord Somers an area of land between the site of St. John's School and Kings Avenue. Here he built two stone cottages and a workshop in which he carried on business as a cordwainer.

Evelyn Saith, who is the great-great granddaughter of William, still lives in St. Johns. In fact, successive generations of the family have lived there for almost two hundred years; living witnesses to the birth and growth of Redhill. But perhaps of more importance, recording snippets of everyday life in a village community.

> "On his death in 1838 his only child, also named William Verrall, inherited the property. He was born in 1813 and became a yeoman farmer, keeping cows and sheep which he grazed on the Common. The cottage had an orchard and a dairy where my great grandmother kept pans of milk and butter. My great grandfather kept the sheep on his land at St. Johns, in a barn at the corner of Kings Avenue and Pendleton Road, or Union Road as it was then".

The family still have in their possession a bell worn by one of the sheep. As his large family grew up, William built the white cottage next to St. John's School and this, together with the original stone cottages, is still standing. Before she died, Evelyn Saith's mother Mabel Shergold who was born in 1884, recalled her early memories and recollections of her grandparents;

> "My grandfather William Verrall was also foreman over digging of sand from the sandpits (on Redhill Common). He died at the age of 78 when I was seven years old

and I can remember him sitting in his Windsor armchair, dressed in a smock and a porkpie hat and smoking a 'churchwarden' pipe. He lived at The Knobb on Earlswood Common and kept cows which were housed in a shed behind his cottage. My mother, when a little girl, used to go to a 'Dame' school in a tiny cottage on the other side of Pendleton Road opposite St. John's School, which is no longer in existence".

The sandpits on the slopes of Redhill Common, where William Verrall worked, were opened-up soon after the construction of the railways. Workings continued, despite considerable opposition, until the "Redhill and Earlswood Commons Regulation Act" was made law in 1884. During the past one hundred years the ugly scars have been covered over by trees and other vegetation. But the steep slopes and deep cuttings mean nothing to the children who play hide and seek, or the owners who now exercise their dogs on Sunday mornings. Only the sign "Sandpit Road" remains a reminder of the past. But the 1884 Act was also effective in curbing the spate of illegal encroachments and "poaching" of Common land, which often went unnoticed as hedges and fences were "pushed" outwards. Not that John Comber was one of these culprits, for he lived at Whitepost Hill and was a most respectable builder. He was also Redhill's first postmaster when his home, which later became part of White Post House, was used as a sub-office to Reigate in 1843. For it was then that the Government of Sir Robert Peel decided that every place where letters received exceeded 100 per week, should be entitled to a receiving office and a free delivery service. However, Mr Comber did not initially provide this service and for several years letters were collected by the recipients themselves.

With the opening of the railway system, the transport of mail by coach and horses from London gradually declined and finally ceased in 1846. This of course spelt the "death knell" for the coaching-inns and one of the first victims was the Somers Arms. But for the Royal Mail and their employees this was a welcome change, as many a journey had been threatened by highwaymen. To counter this threat, every coach had carried a security guard complete with a sword case, which contained a cutlass, brace of pistols and a blunderbuss. He also carried a horn, both to worn other traffic on the road of the coach's presence, as well as the landlords of inns so that fresh horses could be made ready. But though the mail continued to be carried by coaches on some cross country routes, the old coaching days had finally passed into history.

But new history was in the making, as the first signs of development began to take place around the new railway station. There were still problems for the passengers, but as Dr Grece noted, changes were afoot;

> "The South Eastern converted a farm road into an approach road from the top of Redstone Hill, and from the site of the Market Hall westwards. Passengers arriving from Dover or Tonbridge, and bound for Brighton or the south, or vice versa, still had to go, providing their own conveyance from one station to the other, nearly a mile. The indulgence of the Brighton Company relieved them sometimes of this by allowing them to pass along the side of the railway, accompanied by a porter, to carry their luggage. The manifold incovenience and absurdity of this pressed itself so upon the Brighton Company that it came to an arrangement with the South Eastern Company for the use of the latter station for passenger traffic. But there remained one grievance yet. Access to the new station from Reigate and the west was only possible either by going over Whitepost Hill and thence down what is now called the Brighton Road and High Street, or else along the Linkfield Lane to Frenches and southwards. Mr Thomas Dann, who afterwards became the father of the corporation, was the first to accentuate this absurdity. I well remember his speaking to my father that the road which then ended where the Market Field now is, ought to be continued westward to Linkfield Street, and pointing out with his stick the course it should follow, and telling my father that he was canvassing

the directors about it. The road, now Station Road, was made accordingly".

And it must have been with relief that passengers welcomed these improvements. However, though agreement was reached for the joint use of the station, both companies never enjoyed a smooth relationship. There was constant agitation between them and it was not unknown at the new station, for the South Eastern signalman to deliberately hold up the London and Brighton train and let his own one through. The station continued to be known as Reigate until 1849, when a branch line was constructed through Reigate town to Reading. It then was called Reigate Junction until it was rebuilt in 1858 and became Red Hill Junction, before finally changing to Redhill in 1929. Though this first structure was relatively modest, the roof was supported by iron columns which were positioned between the tracks. However, on several occasions these proved lethal for unwary engine drivers, who forgot to keep their heads out of the way. But it took the death of a conductor on a Pullman train before the columns were finally removed in 1895.

The move to extend Station Road westwards heralded the onslaught of a building boom that few could have anticipated. Initially the South Eastern Railway reserved the right of development in their road, where they erected a gate and gatehouse on the site of Lloyds Bank. The gate was kept locked on the first Sunday in every month, to ensure that the private nature of the road was maintained. Upkeep of the road was also carried out by the Company until 1872, when this work was taken over by the Council and the adjoining land sold for building purposes.

However, the influx of scores of workers and others demanded immediate accommodation. In 1846 large areas of land were leased by the trustees of Lord Monson, which extended from Frenchesgate to the bridle path crossing in the High Street and, in the other direction, from Linkfield Street to the railway station. As a result considerable building took place with houses being erected 'cheek and jowl' in Warwick Road, North Street and, to a certain extent, in Station Road and the High Street. Other development was taking place along London Road towards Frenches. Cecil Road and Grove Road were soon to follow, like huge tentacles reaching out from the very heart of what was now called Warwick Town after the Countess Brooke and of Warwick, widow of the fourth Lord Monson. But temporary accommodation was also needed, while the more affluent awaited the construction of their large villas in London Road and Linkfield Lane. Not for them the cheap and nasty terraces that "induce squalor and slum life". And amongst the earliest establishments to meet these needs were the South Eastern Hotel and, to the east of the railway station, The Railway Hotel, later to become Lakers, which was built in 1844. Two years later a licence was granted to Richard Laker "in the Foreign of Reigate, for an Inn, Alehouse or victualling House, at the Sign of the Reigate Junction". Almost immediately he had a copper plate engraved and fitted.

"RICHARD LAKER
REIGATE JUNCTION RAILWAY HOTEL
REIGATE STATION
Neat Wines and Spirits. Post Horses
and carriages for Hire".

Outside the town there was more building. At St. Johns the new National School met the needs of the growing village community, while to the south of Redstone Hill the Philanthropic Society's Farm School opened at its new location in April 1849. Originally founded in 1788 at Southwark, the school catered for almost 300 "convicted" boys, who were grouped into five different houses under the care of masters. Besides attending normal school lessons, the boys worked on the farm and learned a variety of manual trades.

Such was the speed of development in these early years that the conveniences of town life were absent. A good example of this was the location of the post office which remained where it was on Whitepost Hill. Apart from the distance, the track was strewn with potholes and other obstacles, making it highly dangerous after dark. Any request for improvements was ignored, as was the haphazard development, which were constantly fought with opposition from the authorities in Reigate. The fact that the Industrial Revolution was in full swing all over England was of no concern to them. They would rather the area stayed a backwater. From their point of view, the railway and the surrounding developments were an eyesore. Attempts by the developers to introduce lighting and improve roads and drainage were either opposed altogether or, in the case of the latter, grudgingly made in total ignorance of what was required. It was a state of affairs that was to continue for some years before Redhill was accepted as a reality.

Undoubtedly a pioneering atmosphere prevailed and because of it people were determined to stay and "stick it out". In any case conditions were worse elsewhere, for here there was work and the hope of better days ahead. Work, which involved long hours for everyone, including children. For without it they starved or were committed to the Workhouse to earn their keep. But illness was common and many died from simple complaints. Mortality was high amongst infants and young children. And, because of the appalling sanitation or lack of it, dirt was rife and washing themselves a rare occurrence. This uncleanliness prevailed within the houses, which were often infested with vermin. Likewise, bedding suffered the same conditions which continuously bred fleas and other parasites. Even as late as 1880 it was said of people that, "they washed up as far as possible and down as far as possible, but never reached possible".

Living meant working all their lives, even well into their eighties, because there were no pensions. What little money they earned was spent on food and clothes and, in particular, shoes. Sturdy shoes were the essential lifeline that brought them to work in an age when only the wealthy could afford horses and carriages. In the town it was a primitive existence, for they lived in tenements and few had gardens in which to grow vegetables. The working-class could not afford to become sick for there was no welfare state. Until philanthropists addressed the situation later in the century, most people could not afford doctors' fees. As a result bogus and quack doctors made a killing by charging less but rarely curing their patients. Dentists with proper qualifications were rare and, more often than not, painful teeth were extracted with pliers and never filled. Because of the absence of sterile instruments infection was common, though serious body wounds were cauterised with red-hot irons.

Such was life in the early days of Warwick Town, hard and uncompromising, but at least there was work. Families who arrived at the same time all worked, even children under thirteen, provided they did not exceed nine hours. But they no longer worked as chimney-sweeps, for this illegal practice had been banned by Parliament in 1840. Wages were poor but combined family incomes made them considerably better-off than most working-class in the cities at the time. There is no evidence that there were large numbers of destitute people in Warwick Town, though the Workhouse at St. Johns was usually full. By modern standards the conditions left a lot to be desired, but at least they were housed and fed.

And so, too, were the constant influx of visitors who arrived to view the business prospects of the town. For keeping apace with the swift development, the licensing and hotel trades were not slow to meet the demand for accommodation as well as sustinence. Outside the town centre there were a few old coaching-inns, but these were not convenient for the rapidly growing population. By 1854 these needs were being met and in, addition to Lakers Hotel, the Warwick Hotel was offering comfortable accommodation in the town centre. Travellers could still find shelter at the White Lion in Linkfield Street, but thirsts were quicker quenched at The Royal Oak in the High Street or the Thimble and Nutmeg Grater in Warwick Road. But walking to The Royal Oak, which was built on the corner of Grove Road where it joined the High Street, must have been a nightmare in wet weather. For these were the days before the drainage system was laid down and the east side of the High Street was in constant flood. The street itself was often covered in water and a journey to the station meant wading through a virtual lake. The root of the problem was the brook, which flowed past the west side of the station and was uncovered. When two cottages were being constructed in Station Road, work was stopped on the orders of the High Bailiff as it was ...' a place unfit for habitation, being boggy'. In fact before the west side of the High Street had been fully built upon, a deep ditch ran its length from the site of the Wheatsheaf and this was always full of water. Despite these quagmire conditions, Warwick Town was declared by the Government Returns to be, 'the second healthiest place in the kingdom'.

By now business had begun to take a firm grip on the town, which was evidenced by the varied nature of the trades and shops, which were quickly establishing themselves. And one of these was the first estate agent Rees & Company, founded in 1851 by James Rees. He was responsible for much of the early development and, having acquired several leases of land, constructed a number of shops along the west side of the High Street. And not far away, William Whitmore already had premises in Warwick Road and Station Road, from where his dairy supplied milk. Arriving when there were only five cottages in the future town area, he rented meadows from Lord Monson, on land now occupied by Carlton Road and Holy Trinity Church. Over the years the business flourished and by the nineteen fifties was owned by Jersey Dairies. But one of the most successful tradesmen and a future councillor was Walter Arnold, who came to Red Hill, as it was being increasingly referred to, in the early days of development in search of employment. Arriving exhausted, having walked all the way from Handcross in Sussex, he entered a builders shop in Station Road and asked for work. "You get out of here", was the encouraging answer. However, with the aid of a cousin who knew the builder, he applied again the following week and was immediately taken on. In later years he became a master-builder in his own right, when his skills were in constant demand. His business also involved house maintenance and on one occasion, he repaired the painter John Linnell's house on Redstone Hill. He was a distinguished cricketer in his younger days and played with some of the "Greats" at the XYZ Club, whose ground was in the meadows near Gloucester Road. One of these "Greats" was William Caffyn of Reigate, who for many years years was Surrey's greatest batsman and bowler. Considered one of the finest allrounders of his day, he was selected for England and toured Australia on two occasions, the last being in 1862. Two other cricketers to play for Surrey a few years later were G. Comber and E.H. Nice, who lived in Earlswood and were probably associated with Earlswood Cricket Club. Founded in 1858, the Club played their games at The Ring on the Common until they amalgamated with the Redhill club ten years later, to form Redhill Cricket Club. But these were not the only cricketing activities taking place, as anyone wandering over to High Trees would have seen. For here at his home W.B. Waterlow the printer had established his own private club. But only staff or 'honorary members' invited by Waterlow himself could play and the rules drawn up by his head gardener were strict:

      Rule 11 - That any member swearing during play
            be fined twopence.
      Rule 12 - That any member being intoxicated
            during play be fined two shillings
            and sixpence.

But cricket was far from the minds of the builders in 1855 as they hurried to put the finishing touches to The Royal Earlswood Hospital, for the official opening by Prince Albert. Known then as "The Asylum For Idiots" and described as such on old maps, it was established for the "remedial care and education of the feeble-minded". From the outset, the founders agreed that "the care of the idiots should be distinguished from the care of the insane". Among the benefactors was Queen Victoria, who subscribed 250 guineas in the name of the Prince of Wales. By so doing, he became a life member with the "right of presentation of one bed".

The first medical superintendent was Dr John Langdon-Down, who spent ten years here from 1858 and took a compassionate interest in his numerous patients. But the asylum was no sooner open than it became obvious that it would have to enlarged. New wings were built and the extension finally completed in 1872 which could accommodate 600 patients. Over the ensuing years the hospital flourished as an integral part of the local community. Over the years too, the welfare and care of the patients has been foremost, in the dedicated and professional hands of successive generations of nursing staff.

But the welfare of children was also important and in particular education, which without any local authority, was left to the churches and other private bodies to organise. One of the earliest schools was the British School, which used facilities in Warwick Hall, where the YMCA ran a reading-room and library. Soon afterwards an infants' school was opened and this was followed by the Wesleyan School in Warwick Road. Built in 1853 Warwick Hall, which was also known as Holden's Rooms, was used extensively by a number of organisations including a mechanics institute, whose lectures were described as having "enlivened many a writer's Tuesday evenings". All of these activities were designed not only to educate a largely working-class population but also to provide entertainment in what must then have been a rather dull and boring town. Lectures, talks and magic-lantern shows were organised on a regular basis by the YMCA, who on one occasion in 1879 arranged;

"A talk on the Zulus and the Zulu War,
fully illustrated by a splendid
collection of Grand Dioramic Views".

But none of these activities were of any interest to Richard Carrington. Later to become an eminent astronomer, he arrived in Redhill in 1852 and acquired the hillock known as Furze Hill. By the end of the following year he had built a large house surmounted with an observatory, which he called Dome

House. His father, who owned a brewery in Brentford, died suddenly in 1858, forcing Richard to give up his observations of the heavens and take over the business. However, by 1861 he was able to collate his observations and with a grant from The Royal Society, publish them under the title "Observations Of The Spots On The Sun From November 9 1853 To March 1861 Made At Redhill". In 1865 a severe illness seriously affected his work and he had to sell the brewery and his house. He moved to Chart where he built another observatory, but he was dogged by ill-health and eventually died in 1875. Dome House was subsequently demolished and the site is now occupied by blocks of flats.

But Richard Carrington was not the only notable person to make his home in Redhill. For just across the valley on Redstone Hill, John Linnell the celebrated portrait and landscape painter, had built a house overlooking Redstone Hollow in 1852. From here, gazing across the Weald to Chanctonbury Ring in Sussex, he painted many of his most famous works until his death thirty years later. And it was from here too, that he gave away the hand of his daughter Hannah in marriage to Redhill's other painter of renown, Samuel Palmer. Though influenced by Linnell to a certain extent, Palmer was "his own man" and chose to live at Furze Hill House, later The Chantry, Meadvale, until his death in 1881 at the age of 76. The house on Cronk's Hill faced towards Leith Hill and situated close to the Common, must have been an idyllic setting for a painter. But of Redhill town he had other views and in a letter to a friend wrote;

> "Those passing through the ghastly modern town of Redhill, partly a reclaimed swamp, can have no conception of the beauty of some of the scenery not far distant".

And it was to such a destination of beauty that a young boy arrived late one October afternoon in 1854, when the embryo town of Warwick was barely ten years old. But his parents' choice of residence was not amongst the hectic building, noise and grime of the town. Not for them the thunder and smoke of trains, too akin to the suburban life of Bermondsey they had left behind. Rather the ancient hamlet of Linkfield Street, nestling either side of the tree-lined road that reached towards the Common. A village that was still its own, at least for a little longer.

The young lad, Thomas Hooper, was to become one of Redhill's most distinguished architects, as well as a popular speaker on local history. And it was this love of local history that he passed on to his son Wilfred, who also became an acclaimed authority and author on the subject. But Thomas Hooper also had a natural gift of observation and his recollections of the eighteen fifties and his arrival in Redhill, were recalled many years later in the Surrey Mirror. For it is a fascinating glimpse of an age long gone, faded and forgotten in the passage of time; of sleepy village life that knew only the lowing of trudging cattle or the creak of passing carriages; a life where time was unimportant and as yet, undisturbed, untouched by the fingers of urban development.

"The journey was slow and long, and we walked most of the way. It was a fresh experience to us, almost like the entrance into a new life and a new world. Late in the afternoon the van drew up at an old-fashioned house, and before we boys had time to see much, darkness came on, unrelieved by the gas lamps we had been used to. The next day was full of excitement and novelty. The strange house just renovated; the large old-fashioned garden, nuttery, meadow and pond; the tanyard and barns, the people different in look and speech to Londoners.

What was Linkfield Street like in 1854? It was a hamlet, the largest group of houses in the parish except the town of Reigate. Opposite our house was the Fengates Estate with its residence, then old, still standing, and close by, its little farmyard with cottage, barn and sheds. The cottage was occupied by the bailiff, Mr Edward Vigar. His good wife managed the dairy, which supplied milk to the district. They were faithful, worthy folk, who looked after their employer's interests.

South of the Tanyard was an old wooden cottage and above it the village shop kept by Mr Gillham, a newcomer; above that was The White Lion, whose landlord, Stephen Brown, did carting and also kept a little latticed butcher's shop, where a small supply of meat was for sale on Fridays and Saturdays. Adjoining the Inn yard were three cottages. Opposite the inn at the corner of Elms road was a quaint

pair of cottages built on a high bank. They were approached by rustic steps and outside was a draw well. Beneath the cottages was a curious tenement level with the road below. Its internal arrangement seemed to be dark and cavernous, and rather aroused our boyish curiosity, but the old dame who lived there did not encourage archaeological researches.
At the south of these, on the ascent of Redhill, the Common began and facing it was the large cottage with steps, still standing, then some smaller dwellings. In the rear were others facing the common, west. The first off Elms Road, Rose Cottage. Above these were several ancient cottages, one, then adapted for an inn called The Rising Sun, kept by Mr Legg. Higher up and on the common a larger residence (now part of Whitepost House) occupied by Mr Comber, builder and undertaker. Most of these cottages were occupied by natives, whose families had for generations lived in the district.
At the opposite or north end of our street, where it joined Linkfield Lane, crossed by the then new Station Road, were six or seven old cottages, one The Red Lion; also a recently erected inn, the Somers Arms, with a brewery behind. In the meadow between Station Road and Linkfield Street was a small group of farm buildings.
Facing Linkfield Lane, opposite the Red Lion, was a fine old Jacobean or Queen Anne residence, at one time the home of a local family of some note, then let off in tenements and called The Barracks, a name given, it is said, because it was used in 1807 as one of several hospitals for sick and wounded soldiers brought back from the Walcheren Expedition, or some such stupid war that our then rulers indulged in. Even in its neglected state it was a beautiful specimen of fine old work. Oak floors and staircase, hand-turned balusters and carved moulding. The nails used in the building were hand-made by some local blacksmith. The architectural charm of the old mansion comes before me now, and it might have remained, a

choice antiquity, but in 1861 the then owner had it pulled down. Some of the materials were re-used in Donyings Place, built nearly opposite in what had been a walled garden. The little hamlet I have thus described, though so humble and obscure, was the chief town of the 'Borough of Linkfield', and yearly chose a Constable and a Surveyor".

But the obscurity of Linkfield Street was fast fading as the remorseless expansion of the town continued; an ever changing landscape of development that had become unstoppable and almost obscene in its urgency. But it was this very speed of development that was beginning to cause problems. Problems of how to deal with and administer a town that was still not regarded as a town; problems the townspeople themselves would have to solve.

Chapter 5
THE ROOTS OF GROWTH

There is little doubt that the speed with which development took place, was responsible for the problem of sanitation. But this also highlighted the lack of a central administrative authority to deal with it, for in 1859 there were no less than 17 different authorities in the petty boroughs of Reigate, Woodhatch, Linkfield, Hooley, Stanton and Colley. And since each of these boroughs was responsible for their own drainage and road maintenance, there was virtually no co-operation between them. An example of this was in Linkfield, where the logical course for a sewer outlet through Hooley was refused out of hand. But if the speed of development was the cause of the problem, it is also fair to say that it was the catalyst that brought about the formation of a joint Borough Council and as a consequence, a solution to the sanitation problem.

However, neither of these problems were easily resolved, least of all the pain and trauma in forming the Borough Council, which alone is a saga of book length-proportions. For it is a story of bickering and in-fighting that knew no bounds; of petty jealousies, open abuse and countless meetings of acrimony and discord, that were even to "dog" the Council in its formative years. But there were men of vision and two of them who stood "head and shoulders" above the rest were Thomas Dann and Dr Clair Grece. And it was due to their perseverence and determination to get something done, that the Council was eventually formed in 1863 and the problem of sanitation resolved. Their efforts were generally supported by the tradespeople during these difficult years, despite powerful opposition from the Lords Somers and Monson and a number of London businessmen who lived locally.

Meanwhile the phenomenal growth of development continued in Redhill with working-class accommodation a priority. In 1857 The Reigate and Redhill Cottage Improvement Society had been formed to meet such a need and one of their first projects, was to build 31 cottages in Ladbroke Road. However, with the demand for housing came the inevitable increase in the price of land. And there is little doubt that the two principal landowners Lord Somers and Lord Monson made handsome profits. Certainly evidence of rising prices was apparent when the Commons Housing Committee were presented with a detailed report.

> "At Reigate there was a large estate called the Ray(Wray) Park Estate and it sold...for about £35 an acre, but the last sales of land upon that estate have been £1000 an acre...".

Prices fluctuated quite considerably within the Borough and most parts of Redhill were cheaper than Reigate. But Redstone Hill continued to be popular and in 1862 John Linnell bought the land adjoining his property for £10,000.

The majority of the houses built on the new estates, were occupied by the more prosperous section of the working-class, who could afford to live in them. This fact was acknowledged by the Reigate and Redhill Cottage Improvement Society in 1857 at their inaugural meeting.

> "We can build for the artisan and mechanic, not for labourers who only receive twelve shillings or fourteen shillings a week, and who can only afford to pay about two shillings out of it for rent. But if we can take those who are a little above the poorest class and put them into better habitations than they at present occupy, then the lowest classes will have the opportunity of getting into the cottages vacated by those a grade above them and thereby we necessarily benefit both classes".

These sentiments were echoed in business circles, who referred to the "wretched accommodation for the artisan and mechanic which exists at Red Hill". And coupled with the wretched accommodation the urgent problem of sanitation, not only for the householders themselves but for shopkeepers too. For here in the streets water-courses which ran into the brook, were laid with tar barrels or brick culverts and quietly used as open sewers. And in them flowed "all manner of filth", which prompted a doctor to "venture to prophesy that if the cholera again visits this country, it will be felt with great severity in this neighbourhood".

Certainly the conditions must have been appalling for everyone and, if it was possible, even worse for the unskilled labourers and their families. But then unskilled labourers were the lowest form of human life and, according to the ruling classes, "adequately housed as befits their station and their forefathers before them". This was not just a Victorian attitude, but rather an inherited legacy of upper class mentality that the working-classes did not actually want better living conditions. Sadly this attitude was to continue into the twentieth century. But now more voices were being raised and the authorities forced to listen. In a "Report on the Sanitary Conditions of the Labouring Population of Great Britain", a section specifically referred to the Borough of Reigate.

> "The great difficulty is to say at what age brothers and sisters do not sleep together in the same apartment, but generally, until they leave home, be that at ever so late a period: many cottages have but one room, and the whole family sleep in one bed".

However, the writer in the Surrey Guardian in July 1857 did not mince his words, when referring to the "Sanitary State of Warwick Town".

> "It is impossible to say we are not in any danger when we look at the state of Grove Place, so badly drained and so thickly inhabited; four families in one house; a man, his wife and five children in one small room; in another room in the same house, a man with five children, thirteen persons in two small rooms, besides a family in each of the other rooms. The small yard at the back of the house is in a most filthy state. Surely people who pay £18 per annum for their houses, ought to have at least proper drainage. If Sir, we have a Health Committee, the gentlemen belonging to it are answerable for the present state of things".

Whatever the state of the sewers might have been, the general health of the district continued to be good, whether by "luck or divine providence". A doctor commenting in a medical journal at the time concluded that the town was "found to have a low death rate by comparison with the return throughout the country".

In 1863 the relentless efforts of Thomas Dann and Clair Grece were rewarded, when the Privy Council was granted Municipal Borough status with the inhabitants empowered to elect a council comprising 6 aldermen and 18 councillors, presided over by a mayor. For electoral purposes the Borough was divided into Eastern and Western Wards, each returning nine councillors. Western consisted of the old petty boroughs of Reigate, Stanton, Colley and part of Woodhatch, while the Eastern apart from Redhill town included Linkfield, Hooley and the remainder of Woodhatch. This arrangement was far from satisfactory and resulted in jealousy between the two towns. Jealousy which at times was fierce and "tended to split the Council into rival camps actuated by sectional interests". This was emphasised in the first election for a town clerk, when there were two contestants, both solicitors, one living in Reigate and the other in Redhill. But it was Redhill's solicitor Clair Grece who got the job, a post he held until his death in 1905.

This Division of the Borough continued for over thirty years and led to growing resentment from the ratepayers of Redhill, which had completely outgrown its more conservative rival. As a result of the increaing tension, significant changes were made around the turn of the century when six new wards were created, with Redhill receiving three, Reigate two and the sixth being designated as a central liaison ward. It was also a time when the constant in-fighting which had dogged the Council since its inception, was finally laid to rest. But it took a bitter dispute over the location of the permanent headquarters for the Municipal buildings, before the Council could be seen "as working in unison for the betterment of the Borough". And this "happening" was due in no small measure to the efforts of another outstanding mayor, Alderman F.E. Barnes, who held the office on no fewer than six occasions. The welfare of the Borough as a whole, was a principle he adhered to throughout his tenure of office and this was why he was successful. He was a gritty fighter and with the best interests of the community foremost in his policies, he gradually wore down the old prejudices and put an end to the sectional in-fighting of the councillors.

But in the meantime the in-fighting continued, though for a while councillors cast aside their differences as they set about tackling the sanitation problem. It was a major undertaking for such a young Borough, but was eventually completed in 1868 at a cost of £8500. The sewage farm on Earlswood Common became the outfall for the system, after Lord Somers had set aside an area of his estate for the purpose. However, as part of the deal, he insisted that the Council purchase sixteen acres of land forming the top of Redhill Common for recreational use. This was eventually agreed for a price of around £3000.

The period between 1861 and 1871 was meteoric as the population of the Borough increased to 16,000 and, with it, a substantial influx of new traders who acquired premises in and around Station Road and the new Market Hall. Built on the corner of Station Road with London Road, the Market Hall and Assembly Rooms was an imposing building, which owed its origins to a conversation between Mr Allsopp of Cormongers Lane and Henry Fowle, who was a watchmaker. Both felt it was important that the town had a market-place and their proposal was supported by Lord Monson and a number of traders. The Market Hall Company was formed and the building constructed in 1860, to include a corn exchange, assembly rooms for hire and later a library. But the construction was not without probems, as piles had to be driven down to a considerable depth because of the boggy nature of the ground. And this was a feature of most buildings built in the town centre over the area known as the "Rough Moors".

Elsewhere the spiritual needs of the growing town were being met with a spate of church building. But it was this Victorian grimness of churchgoing and the austerity of an average Sunday, that was graphically described many years later in St. John's Parish Magazine by a former choirboy.

"The ancient (sic) building was as bare and unattractive as it could possibly be. There was a gallery for the children attending Sunday School and for the children who came from the Workhouse. The reading desk was on the left-hand side of the apse and on the right a high pulpit. The heating apparatus was very inadequate. There was a fire just inside the west door and another in the aisle. The Church was lighted by two candles placed on the pulpit with frosted shades, two on the reading desk that were seldom used, and two on the small organ in the gallery. The organ was installed in 1850. Prior to that time Mr Dinner, the schoolmaster of St. John's, led the singing of the boys and girls with a tuning fork - not a dinner fork! I have a keen recollection of the length of the services, which were very tedious and sombre, making the Sunday anything but a bright and joyful day. There was never any singing during Lent or Advent, while on the other Sundays only two hymns or portions of psalms were used. There was a celebration of Holy Communion once a month and on the major festivals.

The services were at 11 o'clock in the morning and at 3 o'clock in the winter and 3.30 in summer. The windows in the whole of the Church were plain, with leaded lights, and on the south side were long green curtains, for sometimes the sun would shine through the windows quite brightly. On these occasions Mrs Skilton, the Church cleaner, used to go and draw the curtains as blinds to keep out the sun; as they were suspended from an iron rod with heavy brass rings, she made some considerable noise in performing this office, and generally caused the preacher to make a pause in his sermon. She always gave the Church a thorough spring cleaning every Whitsun. Her husband, known as "Old Jimmy", could make himself heard all over the Church. He used to sit just inside the west door, provided with a long stick, and if he heard anyone talking or noticed anyone sleeping, down came that stick on the unfortunate person's head. It would cause no small commotion among the congregation.

St. John's School, built in 1845, being the only school in the district, was attended by children far beyond its immediate circle - even from Nutfield and Sidlow. It was one of the unwritten laws that the children who attended the Day School must attend the Sunday School. Sunday to the children was a hard and laborious day. School commenced at 9.30am, and we were expected to be word perfect in the Collect, Epistle and Gospel for the day. At 10.45 we were marched from the school to the Church, usually leaving to be home for 1 o'clock dinner. Then at 2 o'clock Sunday School again. From school to Church at 2.45 and we were dismissed at 4.45. Sometimes it was quite dark when we came out of Church, and we were frightened of going home in the dark...The Church was decorated with heavy evergreens for Christmas - it would have been considered a sin to decorate the Church with flowers, but happily today a better atmosphere prevails."

In 1861 the first St. Joseph's Church was built on a site at the corner of the High Street and Chapel Road, largely due to the generosity of Lady Mostyn. She was an ardent Roman Catholic and, in the early years, had arranged services to be held in the loft of her stables at Hooley Lodge. The house was opposite the present site of the gasometers and demolished in later years, to make way for the Hooley Mead development. A year later the Congregational Chapel was also built in Chapel Road and this was followed in 1866, with the consecration of St. Matthew's Church in Station Road. This was recognition of a need for a new parish and it was formed out of the northern part of St. John's. But not all parishioners were happy and complained of, "being throw'd into Warwick".

And perhaps they had good reason, as shops, hotels and pubs sprang up in Station Road, the High Street and the other roads and streets which intersected them. But not just traders, for with growth came the need for the essential services of the police and the fire brigade. Based in Redhill, the first police station was established in 1864 and premises acquired at 3 Carlton Terrace close to the Market Hall. The Superintendent was George Rogers, who made a habit of touring the district in a four-seater pony carriage to emphasise his position. This was also apparent in his attire, as initially he did not wear a uniform and donned a tall hat as an indication of his rank. His salary of £90 per annum, was only marginally better than the eighteen shillings a week earned by his constables including clothing, but at the time considered "fitting to the position". The Headquarters remained in Redhill until 1902 when it was transferred to Reigate. The Borough Police as they were called, continued as an independent force until 1943 when they were absorbed into Surrey County Constabulary. Almost adjacent to them was the Redhill Volunteer Fire Brigade which was formed a year later in 1865, following a public meeting at the Tower Inn. The first equipment and personnel consisted of a manual machine, hose cart, hand carts and truck teams to man them, in addition to a superintendent or captain (a Mr Collins) and twelve firemen. The manual machine ran on heavy wooden iron-bound wheels and was pulled by two or four horses. It consisted of a pair of single-acting force pumps worked by four, six or eight men, which were capable of throwing a jet of water to a height of 100 feet.

But there was also an urgency for other essential services and in particular gas and water. Though gas for lighting had been supplied in Reigate since 1838, the Reigate Gas Company was unwilling to extend its mains to Redhill to supply the needs of the South Eastern Railway. Forced to take action, the Railway built their own gas works near Merstham to light the tunnel and another beside their station in Redhill. These remained in use until the

Redhill Gas Company was founded in 1860, as did several other small Works in the area, including one for the sole use of the Royal Earlswood Hospital. The first committee meeting of the Redhill Gas Consumers Company was held on 2nd December 1859 at The Railway Hotel. The principal item on the agenda was;

> "Decide to make enquiries about the site for a gas works and the likely requirements of consumers".

Amongst other business was a decision "to pay Mr Laker of The Railway Hotel, £3 per year for the use of a room for the directors of the Company".

A site was selected just off the Brighton Road on land now occupied by Henly Ford and other businesses and a gasometer, buildings and yards constructed. But it was not until 1865 that the Company was incorporated by Act of Parliament, with a capital of £50,000 and a mortgage limit of £12,500, for the purpose of supplying gas to, " the inhabitants of Warwick Town and Redhill in the Foreign of the Parishes of Reigate and its neighbourhood". Though authorised to supply gas to Reigate as well, the Company came to an arrangement by which they agreed, "in perpetuity not to supply gas in that portion being supplied by the Reigate Company". The original clauses in the Redhill 1865 Act also empowered the Company to supply water to the neighbourhood, but these were withdrawn upon an assurance by the Caterham Spring Water Company, that they would undertake to meet the needs of the community.

Initially gas was only used for lighting and the Act laid own certain standards to be observed;

> "The gas should be of such illuminating power as to produce from an Argand burner having fifteen holes and a seven inch chimney, and consuming five cubic feet of gas per hour, a light equal in intensity to the light produced by 14 sperm candles of six to the pound burning 120 grains per hour".

Eager to attract investors and presumably customers in its formative years, the Redhill Gas Company were quick to emphasise the potential of the town. Though formed in 1860 it was to be another five years before business became profitable. But by then the doubts of earlier years had faded and the company were able to pay a ten percent dividend, with its £5 shares being quoted at £12.

> "The delightful scenery of this neighbourhood, its salubrious atmosphere and the facilities of transit to and from the metropolis are now becoming generally appreciated; and the result of this is that a large number of magnificent residences have recently been erected in all directions; and we understand that in the course of the ensuing summer (1861), many acres which are now used for pasture, will be covered with handsome buildings, or converted into pleasure grounds. Redhill and the neighbourhood, in fact, bids fair to become not only a place of great commercial importance but also one of the most fashionable suburbs of London. Its future prosperity must however, depend, in a great measure, on the inducements which are held out to Capitalists and Millionaires to settle here".

An interesting prediction even if the millionaires are still in short supply, but thankfully wrong about becoming a suburb of London.

The extension of the Caterham Spring Water Company's mains to Redhill in 1867 must have been the height of luxury for a community that, until then, had relied on wells and water carts. A community that at last was to have its dead respectfully laid to rest by a caring firm of undertakers. For it was during these years that John Stoneman, who had earlier been employed as a carpenter and cabinet maker, decided to open his own business. Acquiring premises in Brighton Road opposite Brook Road, he opened up as an undertaker, cabinet maker and upholsterer. The business prospered and in the 1880's Stonemans moved to Cromwell Road, where they had stables for the horse-drawn hearses and carriages, as well as buildings to carry out their work as monumental masons and letter-cutters. At about the same time they opened a showroom at 100 Station Road and it was from here that they continued to operate for many years.

Meanwhile the railways were flourishing as they met the demands of a growing band of commuters, as well as the continual arrival of new residents. Demands which they met in Earlswood in 1868, with the construction of a new station and additional trains of 3rd class wagons, packed with "the poorer elements enjoying cheap excursions to the Seaside; eight hours in Brighton". But it was not just passengers that the railways sought, as freight services increased and facilities for the Royal Mail and banks were provided. For with the demise of the stage-coaches the Royal Mail transferred much of their business to this faster form of transport. And so did the banks and other business houses. However, the masterminds in the criminal world were not slow to attempt robberies. Aware of the dangers, the railway companies provided secure vans and a system which thwarted most attempts. But in 1855 one robbery was successful and was later referred to as "The First Great Train Robbery". The target was a consignment of gold bars which were being transported to the continent, using the South Eastern Railway. And it was soon after the train had passed through Redhill that the robbery took place. By gaining access to the security wagon, the thieves substituted the gold bars with lead and threw their haul to waiting accomplices by the side of the line.

It was a daring robbery but one that probably went unnoticed by the majority of people in Redhill. For they were too occupied with building and trading to notice; too occupied with local "happenings" to take note of outside events; and too occupied as the new Reigate and Redhill Cottage Hospital was completed in 1866. For their lives were now firmly entwined with Redhill, as they nurtured the roots of the businesses they had founded.

Looking towards St. Annes from Copyhold Cottages in the early 1900s. (courtesy Mr. Taylor)

The Redhill Manual Fire Brigade often could not answer calls immediately, since it took time to assemble horses and appliances. Prior to 1890, it was common practice for local chimney sweeps to advertise their services for extinguishing fires. (courtesy E. Freeman)

ST. JOHN'S CHURCH FROM THE COMMON.

Before it was substantially rebuilt and a new tower and spire added in 1895. William Verrall's old stone cottage is in the centre. (courtesy D. Saith)

Chapter 6
THE VICTORIAN LEGACY

In a sense the pioneering days had passed and with them much of the haphazard building and expansion that had marked the early years. Whatever its faults, there was now a central body to look after the welfare of the town and control development into the suburbs. It meant introducing a semblance of order into the chaos of former years; ensuring that the new roads and buildings of suburban Redhill were better laid out and pleasing to the eye. But of more importance, ensuring that the standard of all types of housing was of better quality than the slum-like structures in the town centre.

If anything, the next thirty years was to witness a building boom of enormous proportions, as the magnet that was Redhill drew in even greater numbers of residents and traders. A period of expanding small companies and entrepreneurial opportunities that had known no equal; a Victorian legacy of bricks and mortar that sadly no longer grace the town centre, yet are still here one hundred years on; proud houses solid and weathered, standing tall, untouched, in Ranelagh Road.

And standing relatively untouched too in Shrewsbury and Brownlow roads, where the United Land Company built them in 1869 and then moved north of the town ten years later, to develop Monson Road Estate. One of a number of companies to recognise the need for orderly building, as did the National Freehold Land Society when they were formed to assist lesser well-off members of the community purchase property. As a result, the Society acquired land from the London, Brighton and South Coast Railway and laid out Bridge, Grove Hill and Ridgeway roads. And they did not stop there, for Woodlands Road followed along with developments at Meadvale. It was as one observer remarked, "a sea of activity" and not likely to pass unnoticed by the casual visitor. Certainly this was the case according to a report in 1876, which concluded;

> "When Redhill was made a first class station
> of the Brighton and South Eastern Railways,
> its convenience of access and the charm of
> the scenery, drew it numerous merchants and
> men of business who prefer luxury at a

> moderate distance from the capital. It was of course speedily marked as a quarry by the speculative builder, and on the hill top has grown up a populous railway town of hideous brick shops and habitations, and around it a belt of ostentatious villas, comfortable looking mansions and tasteful and ornate dwellings of many varieties with a super abundance of builders' detached and semi-detached malformations".

A classic touch of flowering Victorian journalism!

Though the hectic building of the earlier years was not quite so apparent in the town, wherever space could be found, there was room for another building or loft. And this was certainly true of pubs and ale-houses, which appeared at most street corners and even between houses. In Station Road the Sussex Arms, which was close to the new post office, was directly opposite St. Matthew's Church and an obvious enticement to the menfolk on Sunday mornings.

But it was the evil of drink that was foremost in many people's minds, as they strove to ensure that none of the notorious "gin palaces" of London, were allowed to be set up in the town. And they went out of their way to make certain they were not, by building temperance hotels and holding meetings that preached sobriety. One of these meetings was organised by the Church of England Temperance Society in December 1878 at the Market Hall, which was well advertised, including a liberal offering of tea. They were becoming concerned about the increase in drunkenness on the streets and felt that urgent action was needed. And so too did the Bishop of Guildford and a cross-section of churchmen and residents.

Reporting on the gathering, The Monthly Illustrated Magazine concluded;
> "Mr W.H. Heaton mentioned that the Society was not confined to total abstainers, but was open to the friends and practisers of temperance in every form. Dr Walters dealt with the medical aspect of the question, condemning the use of alcohol as unnecessary for people in good health".

Whether there was a decrease in drunkenness is not recorded, but the temperance fraternity cannot have been too pleased to read the newspapers a few days later.

> "John Moor, landlord of the Cottage of Content at Merstham, was taken before the Mayor and Sir Valentine Fleming and fined one shilling and sixpence costs, for being drunk while in charge of a horse and cart at Redhill".

Nor would they have been happy to learn that one of the guardians against drunkenness in the streets, had himself "fallen by the wayside". For PC Joseph Harker, with a previous unblemished record, was "regrettably led astray by the vices of alcohol". As an example to others he was "dismissed from the Borough Police, and George Willis, a beershop keeper in Linkfield Street, fined 2/6d and costs, for having harboured the man on his premises whilst on duty".

Not good examples to set the public. But these actions seem to have had no effect on the booming licensing trade, which continued to open new public houses. However, the law was keeping a close eye on developments and another landlord was soon in trouble being,

> "fined twenty shillings for allowing gaming in his house, the gaming consisting of raffling a rabbit belonging to a little boy who lives next door to the inn. We trust that the energetic police constable who detected this flagrant crime will be duly promoted".

And pubs were again in the news a couple of weeks later, when several publicans were fined for, "adulterating their gin with water".

If highlighting drinking and gambling vices was not enough, the evils of smoking were added to the list. Though smoking was considered an enjoyable habit for most Victorian gentlemen, there were some who did not agree. Dr Martin of Reigate was one of them and made his feelings perfectly clear when addressing the Mechanics' Institute.

> "I am willing to hope that none of you are, or ever will be, addicted to the odious habit of smoking. Tobacco is one of the most virulent poisons in nature and though not immediately fatal - it may not kill today, nor tomorrow, but intends to induce diseases of the brain and nervous system.....and thereby shortens life. A man is

> at liberty to smoke in his own house....but in the streets you see ill-behaved and impudent men marching along and puffing their filthy smoke in the faces of people they meet....and defiling the pure atmosphere which others wish to breathe".

However, despite these worrying signs, the annual August railway excursion in 1879 organised by the Reigate and Redhill Band of Hope, went ahead as usual. Unfortunately the organisers' misgivings were justified and events did not turn out as they had planned. And considering the numbers involved it was not altogether surprising. For that year two trains set off for Portsmouth with 1300 residents, to enjoy the sights of the harbour and the music of a military band. According to a local newspaper report a number of the day-trippers behaved rather badly which, reading between the lines and restraints of Victorian journalism, meant they got very drunk.

> "There were some few, evidently not members of the Band of Hope, who cared for none of (the sights of Portsmouth), and whose idea of enjoyment was not by any means an elevating one - rather the reverse; and for such, Portsmouth, it was quite clear, had afforded abundant gratification, for long before the time arrived for returning, they evinced a decided tendency to go on all fours".

Certainly Dr Clair Grece and his wife would not have approved of this behaviour, but then they were pre-occupied with other matters. And in particular checking on the sewage farm on Earlswood Common, which had become a favourite destination for walkers. One which was popular with the good doctor and his wife, who obviously did not have sensitive noses.

> "June 3rd - Dr Grece and self walked to the bottom of Earlswood Common to look at the drainage works. Gossiped with a workman and his wife who are living in a cart near the works".

Perhaps the sewage works was a good example of people co-operating for the welfare of the community. But regrettably none of this co-operation was demonstrated within the Council itself, which continued to be beset with petty jealousies and strife; and with class distinction. For in the early years of free vote elections, the composition of the Council still tended to be biased towards "gentlemen", retired army or navy officers and the professional classes. It was true that working men just did not have the time to sit on councils, but class distinction still existed generally. The few that did get elected were made to feel uncomfortable by their 'betters'. A newspaper commenting on the defeat of a candidate concluded;

> "....though he was an honest, well meaning,
> upright man of business, he could not meet
> the bulk of the other members of the Council,
> feeling that he was on an equality with them"

And a Redhill resident writing the The Monthly Illustrated Journal in 1878 observed;

> "The great vice of many corporations as it is of
> many individuals, is selfishness. Selfishness
> begets jealousy, and jealousy is a great hindrance
> to public business. Now selfishness can
> spoil a class as well as an individual".

He was sad to see that certain individuals of the "upper social classes", were still clinging to power as if it was "their birthright".

> "Look at the constitution of the Council: it is of
> such a kind as to encourage displays of petty
> jealousy. A Borough, with a population of over
> 16000, divided alas! Literally DIVIDED into two
> Wards for the purpose of Local Government: the
> Tycoon of Reigate, the Mikado of Red Hill. Here
> is an instance of that senseless clinging to a
> (class position) because it was originally so".

There may well have been a reluctant acceptance that all men were born equal, in the context of democratically electing councillors. But then the upper echelons of Victorian society would have added...'but some men are born more equal than others'.

Not that Edward Lambert who owned the Blackborough Mill and a bakery shop in the High Street was one of them. For though elected mayor in 1879 he was not popular with some councillors, who did not consider a miller was the right sort of person to hold that office. It was difficult enough for gentlemen to sit and talk with "commercial people"; it was positively unthinkable to have one higher up the public ladder than them. But times were changing and Edward Lambert was so popular with the ratepayers that he was elected for a second term. And no doubt continued to live with his family in their modest house beside the mill.

Meanwhile the townspeople carried on with their lives, happy that at least something was being done, even if the policymakers were content to squabble and bicker. Most enjoyed the Saturday market which stretched the length of the High Street from the Whitesheaf. Apart from the usual stalls, there were from time to time additional "attractions" such as, "a travelling cheap-jack selling crockery, a quack doctor retailing a 'cure-all' physic (medicine) and a strongwristed dentist extracting teeth publicly".

For others 1879 was a significant year with the launch of The MidSurrey Mirror, the fore-runner of The Surrey Mirror. An earlier paper The Reigate and Redhill Express had been produced in January 1873 by Joshua Brackett of Station Road, but was short-lived and finally ceased publication about a year later. But the Weekly Illustrated Journal continued to keep people informed of local happenings. In particular they were delighted to read of,

"....satisfaction that the South Eastern Railway Company
are about to give up making their own gas for the supply
of Redhill Station, and will therefore, it is presumed,
remove the works which have, for a long period, offended
people's noses if not their eyes".

There were other items in the news too, though hardly major headlines. For appearing before local magistrates, "one George Norbury, a little boy, was fined 2/6d and 5/- costs, for throwing stones in Woodlands Road". And this was a lot of money for a young boy in 1879, but stone-throwing on public highways was a very serious offence. On a happier note, as the new decade dawned, a group of people leased a plot of land between Linkfield Lane and Carlton Road and formed the Redhill Croquet and Lawn Tennis Club. By 1918 the croquet activities had virtually ceased, but tennis flourished and in 1951 the Open Junior Tournaments were officially recognised by the Lawn Tennis Association.

Though advertising products and services had been in use for centuries, it was not until the late nineteen hundreds that almost every newspaper, journal and even books carried advertisements of some description. This was particularly relevant in Redhill, as older-established businesses became aware of the continual influx of new competitors. And not just the threat of competition, for new residents had to be made aware of these trusted and reliable business houses. Even John Stoneman and Sons took to advertising, for they recognised a new market. While the relatives of the rich could well afford to send their "dearly departed off in the grand manner", it was not so for the average working family. Expensive oak-lined coffins and all the trimmings of a grand funeral were just not affordable. But Stonemans were aware of the financial difficulties many families had and were able to offer an affordable funeral. The coffin was of ordinary wood, secured with nails rather than brass hinges and handles. The cost was £4.5/- with an additional charge of nine shillings, if the relatives required the services of a gravedigger.

But it was at the living that advertising was directed. For here in Station Road, children attending St. Matthew's Schools could buy milk for a penny a glass at the Ham Farm Dairy shop. And further down the road musically-minded Arthur Woods, was offering pianos for twentyone guineas or 10/6d " if hired by the month". Not far away F.S. Sillitoe the chemist, assured the public that;

"Sillitoe's Digestive & Stomach Pills, a certain remedy
for indigestion, wind etc.
Sillitoe's Scurf Cream is a real cure for Scurf or
Dandriff.(sic)
Sillitoe's Toothache Tincture, most effectual
application to decayed teeth.
Sillitoe's Soothing Liniment, invaluable in
Rheumatism, Gout, Spasm etc.
Sillitoe's Powders for Children, are known
everywhere and recommended by all for the good".

In an age when most people paid cash for their purchases, some traders obviously had doubts and were taking no chances.

"CHAS. MANNING - DRAPERS, High Street

Cheapest and best value in the trade.
But Business Conducted Strictly on the
Ready-Money Principle and Definitely -

'NO CREDIT'".

This principle was probably practised by Walter Arnold in Brighton Road, a man of many skills; "Plumber, Painter, Gasfitter, Glazier and House Decorator".

But not everyone advertised in the newspapers, least of all the Muffin Man; for he did his own as he plied the streets of the town, balancing a tray full of muffins and crumpets on his head and ringing a bell to attract customers. Not that he really needed to, with the dense crowds that attended the brass band concerts on Tuesday evenings in Marketfield. Or that memorable occasion in 1884 when there was another Royal Visit. An occasion for which the people of Redhill had waited three long years, since the land had been purchased on the east side of the station from Redstone Manor and Wiggey Estate.

For here the Royal Asylum of St Anne's had slowly taken shape; a vast Victorian structure that was soon to tower over the town. A landmark not just for Redhill, but for the St. Anne's Society itself who had, since 1702, been educating and clothing children,"whose parents had become reduced in circumstances" Now with accommodation for 150 girls and 200 boys, it was fitting that this impressive building should be opened by someone of importance.

The 9th July was another warm and fine day, in a summer that had been above average. A day which brought out most of the population and certainly all of the press.

By now it was clear that Redhill and its suburbs was as ideal a setting for institutions, as it was for those who had come to stay. It was popular too for day-trippers, boating on the lakes, or just making official visits, as Florence Nightingale did with her wooer Richard Monkton Milnes to the Philanthropic School. In a letter to a friend she wrote;

> "He (Monkton Milnes) had the same voice and manner
> for a dirty brat as for a duchess...once at Redhill,
> the Reformatory, when we were with a party and the
> chiefs were telling us the system in the middle of
> the courtyard, a mean,stunted, villainous - looking
> boy crept across the yard (quite out of order) and
> stole his dirty paw into Mr Milne's hand. He stayed
> quiet and contented if he could touch his benefactor".

But not all parts of Redhill were ideal and picturesque and the sandpits on Redhill Common were amongst them. However, as a result of the threats of legal action by a number of gentlemen including Samuel Barrow, who owned the Tannery and had grazing rights on the site, the excavations eventually came to an end. And this coincided with Royal Assent and the 1884 Act of Parliament, that opened up common land to the public. It was almost too late, but at least it put an end to the long years of encroachment. A practice that had been encouraged by the so-called "Surrey Custom". This effectively had made an allowance of three feet outside the boundary hedge or fence, as the actual boundary of the property. In one recorded instance, a man had loosened the base of a bank with the hedge on it. Then when the opportunity arose, he placed timber along the inside and with a screw-jack, pushed bank and hedge intact several feet on to the common.

Now after centuries of private use by the Lords of the Manor, the commons were freely available to the public and worthy of mention in a guidebook of the time.

"The disappointment experienced in some hilly
districts whose hilltops are inaccessible to the
public, will not be felt here.
A short walk and the breezy waste is reached.
The surroundings are very unartificial and no
rules are enforced, but such as are desirable
to check mischief and rowdyism".

Not that rowdyism was in the minds of old farmhands when cattle and sheep grazed there. Rather a knowledgable eye cast at the sky and words of wisdom for anyone who cared to listen;

"if on a damp, uncertain morning the sheep
go up Red Hill, it foretells a fine day".

But the weather was far from people's thoughts when a dog with rabies was found on Wray Common acting strangely. It was immediately taken to Redhill Police Station and shot, but unfortunately the animal had already bitten a 16-year-old boy. Such was local concern that he was sent to the Pasteur Institute in Paris and all expenses were paid by the Council. But it was concern of a different kind people had in 1881, when a young boy who was to become known in later life as "The Devil's Disciple" of black magic arrived in Redhill with his parents. The house they came to live in until 1885 was The Grange, which was off Frenches Road in heavily wooded grounds. And it was here in the grounds that the boy Aleister Crowley, who was to call himself "Beast 666", prepared for his future life of debauchery and evil. Even at this early age, he would lie in wait at the end of the garden and ambush children on their way to school in Merstham. And it became such a regular occurrence, that the children were forced to take another route to school.

But by 1887 Aleister Crowley had departed and in any case, the undulating turf of Earlswood Common was of more interest to Charles Hall and his friends. Not just for walking on, but for hitting golf balls across and thinking of the prospects of a Club. And a year later this became a reality, when permission was given for the Redhill and Reigate Golf Club to form provided, "due care was taken when the public were out walking and occupied in other pursuits". And no doubt they did, but on November 5th 1891 the public were elsewhere on Redhill Common enjoying the annual carnival. An occasion which the organisers, the Redhill Torchlight Society described in their programme as, "The Annual Carnival....a night in Fairyland, or Redhill as it should be". It was certainly spectacular and boasted 3000 torches in a procession which included floats and several local bands. A procession which wound its way through the streets before reaching the Common and the highlight of the event, a bonfire and fireworks display. It was a memorable event which always attracted large crowds from the Borough and surrounding districts but sadly was discontinued around the turn of the century.

In 1891 an extension was built to the Market Hall, which included another meeting-room to meet the growing demand for facilities. To celebrate the occasion a "grand dinner" was held and diners could make a choice of saddle leg and boiled mutton, roast beef, veal and ham, fowl and York ham, or pheasant and jugged hare. The popularity of the Market Hall was not just confined to the Redhill Society of Instrumentalists, who had made it their venue since the previous year. It was also the permanent address of the Capital and Counties Bank until 1901, when they moved to the present Lloyds Bank building. Another permanent resident was the Post Office which occupied the west wing, before moving to London Road in 1932.

Though it might be presumed that the post office had some connection with the telephone service, this was not the case in the early years of the National Telephone Company. In fact for a period the local exchange was operated from Rees and Company's office in Station Road. Apart from their estate agency duties, calls to and from Redhill subscribers were dealt with by the staff. Since the number of subscribers at the time were only seven, the additional work burden cannot have been very great. In the circumstances no night service was offered and the exchange closed down each day at 7pm. Among these early subscribers was Hall and Company in Brighton Road, who allowed customers to use the phone for one shilling a call. But a lady who drew up in a carriage and pair outside Quinton's furniture store one day, had other ideas. She asked if she might use the telephone. Permission was granted and she rang up a London firm of furniture dealers and asked them to come down and take up her carpets for beating. It is not recorded what the local furniture dealer said!

The substantial rebuilding of St. John's Church which began in 1889 and continued for six years, was a love of labour resulting in the beautiful building that is today the most striking feature of Redhill's skyline. But during these long years of toil, not everything went according to plan. For one labourer, who was working on the level the spire had reached, started to come down but then lost his nerve. He simply could not move and had to have his dinner sent up. Eventually his mates had to tie a rope under his armpits and lower him down by stages, from one platform to the next, until he had reached the ground. On another occasion a bucket suspended near the top of the spire was found one morning to contain a hedgehog that was very much alive. The mystery remained unsolved although a local policeman was thought to be the culprit.

For the residents of St. Johns the building of the new steeple was quite an event. Many years later Mabel Shergold recalled those days of hectic activity.

> "I also remember the church tower being built
> and hearing the bells when they first chimed.
> An uncle of mine helped in the building of it.
> Two little boys who lived near, pulled a stone
> over on them and were killed. They are buried
> in the churchyard".

But apart from this tragedy life continued to be peaceful at St. Johns, as young Mabel grew into her teens towards the turn of the century.

"St. Johns was a lovely quiet place; the air was fresh and clean, with poppies in the cornfield and bluebells and primroses growing in the copse. I was born in a little cottage near the barn and went to St. John's School when I was 2½ years. It was compulsory to go at three years. There was no footpath up to the school then.

My friend Grace Harinden lived near. There was no water laid on, so it had to be fetched from a well. Her brother Alf used to come down with a yoke on his shoulders and two buckets. They had no kitchen, just four rooms. Later a small cupboard was fixed near the well and a tap put there. A little way from the well was a brick shed where Alf used to do shoe mending - that has all been pulled down, the well filled in and a bungalow built. Close to our house was a big black gate and the barn where the sheep used to stay at night. And the old shepherd used to sleep in there too. We kept lots of chickens and they used to run on the Common. We had a nice garden with sheds and a chicken house. I used to take eggs round to different houses for 10d per dozen. Kings Avenue was a funny little place - very few old cottages and a Public House called The Brickmakers Arms. Later these old places were pulled down and Mr Viall, a councillor, had the present houses built.

The Elmshades has been there ever since I can remember and behind it was a little cottage. In front of that was a little hut where a Mr Hall used to do shoe mending. These places have all disappeared, likewise The Fountain public house - that has gone. On the green below St. John's Church there used to be a pump. I can also remember one

Saturday evening when I was quite young, the St. John's laundry caught fire and the sparks came over our house. I was very frightened and the fire engine with two horses came galloping down the road. I was nearly ten years old when I saw the first motor go down the road. It was a Brougham like a closed carriage without shafts, with a coachman and a footman sitting up in front wearing top hats. It was slow and made no noise. Of course there were also horses and carriages and the huntsmen and their dogs.

As a child I used to go across the road to Jeremiah Hawkins' shop in Little London, to get a halfpenny of sweets in two packets for my sisters. Sometimes I would get ½oz of tobacco for my father for a penny three farthings and I would have the farthing change. We often had to take a basin over there for 2d worth of jam or treacle, or run over the Common to the farm for a quart of milk in a can for 4d. We used to go to Redhill to get 6d worth of meat from Coopers in Cromwell Road. I always remember large sides of pork and bacon hanging in the scullery or cupboard, and also mother used to have large crocks of lard. She used to work very hard in those days, everybody did, but we could walk anywhere alone in safety and there was no need to lock the door at night".

But Mabel Shergold was not the only person to see a "horseless carriage" as the eighteen nineties drew to a close, even if they were few and far between. In fact there were several of them as the Surrey Mirror reported on 17th November 1896.

"THE MOTOR CAR - THE INAUGURAL RUN

A few minutes after noon the large crowd which

had gathered at the junction of High Street with Station Road, received the news that the motors had passed Croydon. Thirty minutes later they witnessed the first arrival - a motor which entered Redhill at a rate of less than 14 miles per hour".

A stirring occasion for young children to remember, but not quite as memorable as the celebrations to mark Queen Victoria's Diamond Jubilee on June 22nd the following year. For as the Surrey Mirror noted;
"By the oldest as well as the youngest inhabitants of the Borough of Reigate, the day will always be held in vivid recollection. The people of Reigate and Redhill rose to the occasion in a manner that betokened that Her Majesty has no more loyal subjects than those in this Borough".

The actual celebrations consisted mainly of dinners for the less well - off, to which appropriately those of sixty years of age or more were invited. One of these dinners was held at the Market Hall, with the catering arrangements in the capable hands of Mr E.J. Hammett of the Warwick Hotel. Amongst the outdoor activities was the opening of the Sports Ground to the public, where an "enjoyable afternoon was spent by a large gathering". In the evening there was a torchlight procession to the top of Redhill Common where "a great bonfire was lighted".

But the occasion must have been touched with nostalgia too, at least for the older generation that day. For surely here was a reminder that the last years of Victorian Redhill were drawing to a close and with them, the passing of an older way of life.

Chapter 7
A QUICKENING TEMPO

The dawn of the new century did not bring with it any immediate or noticable changes to life in Redhill, or indeed in any part of England. Queen Victoria still reigned, surrounded by an aging Court clinging, as it were, to the last fading moments of the only way of life they had known. An older generation unwilling to submit to, or accept, the changes that were subtly taking place around them. Changes brought about by the "new-fangled" inventions of a younger generation, the effects of which even they could not have foreseen. Inventions that included the telephone, the combustion engine and electricity;inventions guaranteed to modernise the old ways and propel society into a brave new world that was effectively a second industrial revolution.

But within a year the brave new world had arrived as Queen Victoria's long reign finally came to an end. It was as if a great mantle of grimness and all things prim and proper had been suddenly lifted. A release from the strict moral attitudes and dark dress that had epitomised Victorian England society. For now there was colour and song and new fashions. New attitudes of behaviour too, as young couples strolled hand in hand un-chaperoned, oblivious to the disapproving glances of the older generation. Aging, watery eyes that stared at them resigned, yet not accepting their radical attire. Tall, slender girls in elegent dresses accentuating waistlines, with escorts, clean-shaven, sporting multi-coloured blazers and boaters. Fashions that were the hallmark of the new age.

And it was this new generation, this new society,that galvanised itself into a veritable frenzy of activity. A quickening tempo of activity, the like of which Redhill had never seen before. Not just construction, though the imposing new buildings at the Crossroads gave the town character; nor the fresh influx of people who brought a variety of trades and skills with them; but rather the influence electricity, the motor car and their related industries were to have on the whole infrastructure of life. Changes, which in 1901 brought a widening of the station tunnel often referred to as "the death trap" and the Reading Arch Bridge, to meet the considerable increase in road traffic. For here at least was agreement between the Council and the South Eastern Railway, both recognising that increased traffic meant additional business for everyone. The fact that the two railways were still at loggerheads came as no surprise to anyone, least of all their passengers.

In a booklet of the period, the author was far from complimentary on the operations of both the South Eastern Railway and the London and Brighton. Of the South Eastern he remarked that;

> "....it has failed to earn a reputation
> for undue haste in its movements".

A sentiment echoed by the long-suffering public, now utterly sick of this continual battle between the two companies.

> "The two lines inconvenience each other
> at all times and seasons".

And Burridge the author of the booklet would have known, since he was a regular passenger between Earlswood and Redhill on the London and Brighton evening train.

> "I have grown quite familiar with the luggage train
> wherewith the South Eastern Railway blocks the line
> about the time my train is expected. That nothing
> happens of a serious nature is probably due to the
> signalman but....so many things, apparently unaccountable,
> are done at the Redhill Junction, that I humbly venture
> to suggest without irreverence, that a special Providence
> watches over the antics of the rival companies and
> averts, the disaster ordinary mortals look upon as but
> a question of time....(perhaps) when the South Eastern
> Railway directors wake up...Redhill Junction will be
> improved and the station,famous for its constant supply
> of fresh air in the windy season, may cease to furnish
> its proverbial coughs and colds to passengers".

But at least the London, Brighton and South Coast Railway had made an effort for progress, by constructing a double track line from just north of Coulsdon to the junction with the Brighton line at Hooley Lane. To reach this point the so-called Quarry Line as it became known, travelled south from Merstham, under Redstone Hill and across by the goods yard. It was, they assured the public, to provide a faster route to the south coast and relieve pressure at Redhill Station. Pressure not only from daily commuter traffic, but weekend passengers too, who flocked in for the market and the occasional football match at the Sports Ground.

And what a magnificent green oasis the Memorial Sports Ground was, left as it had been in trust, ".....for the people of the Borough and for the use by the senior football team". A ground beautifully designed and laid out by Leonard Rees the grand-nephew of James Rees; designed with the same care for detail that he had shown with other buildings in the town. For he was a man of many talents, not least among them being a chess player of international class, capable of taking part in twenty games simultaneously.

Perhaps the most significant event to effect everyone in the course of time, was the connection of the electricity supply to the town in May. For the first six weeks the supply was free, as the Council was keen to attract as many customers as possible. And one of the first of these consumers was the landlord of the New Inn in Brighton Road. Thrilled as he must have been by flicking a switch, his excitement would not have extended to the erection of the new gasholder in Hooley Lane about the same time. Unwelcome perhaps, but necessary for the needs of a growing community, as had been the opening of the Isolation Hospital for infectious deseases at Whitebushes in March.

But there was also concern that year as the police moved their headquarters to Reigate. Concern which grew when a lunatic, armed with a razor, made a violent attack on two policemen injuring them both and then dying within minutes, after cutting his own throat. Concern too for the increasing numbers of vagrants unable to be accommodated in the Workhouse. A sad reflection on the poverty that just would not go away. Now it was necessary to board them in 'common lodging houses' in Grove Road, where they were given food and a little money in return for domestic duties. There were two types, those who were 'travelling vagrants' and local ones. The 'travellers' were moved on as soon as possible, usually to the next workhouse in Epsom. The 'locals' continued to operate around the town and would often be seen street-singing or begging.

Not that they would have been carrying out these activities anywhere near Nicol's brand new Drapery and Furniture Stores at the Crossroads on 25th May. For within a matter of hours, this prestigious building, which stood opposite the Wheatsheaf, had been reduced to smouldering rubble by the greatest fire the town had ever experienced. Breaking out soon after 1pm, the fire is believed to have been caused when a flapping curtain came into contact with a gas lamp. Such was the intensity of the flames fanned by a north-east gale, that no fewer than thirteen other fires broke out elsewhere in the town, as a result of flying embers and sparks. At one stage the upper floors of the Wheatsheaf caught fire, as did the breast pocket handkerchief of a gentleman in the High Street. But the combined efforts of several fire brigades from as far afield as Croydon and Horsham, were able to stop the fire spreading along Station Road. However, Nicols was left a charred and twisted ruin, mourning the loss of two of its staff. The efforts of the fire brigades came in for considerable praise, particularly from the newspapers;

> "But for their work and the intelligence with which they directed their operations, the result to Redhill would have been of the most disastrous and devestating character. They worked hard and with a will".

The subsequent inquest brought to light several shortcomings in dealing with fires, the most serious being the delay before the fire brigade was ready to respond. The coroner suggested that a searching enquiry should be held by the local authorities, to see if improvements could be made in calling together members of the fire brigade and as to the efficiency of the fire appliances. It seemed to him that the procedure of a police constable calling on individual members of the brigade was somewhat antiquated. "Surely", he argued, "now that telephones were much in use, the time had come when every member should be in direct contact with the police station, or as an alternative, a siren could be used".

It was tragic that a catastrophic fire of this nature had to happen, especially as the recent invention of the telephone could have played such an important part in saving lives. But it would be some years yet before Victorian thinking and old methods of doing things were finally laid to rest. At least the new fire station being built in Reigate with sliding poles and electric lights would be a vast improvement. In the meantime life must go on and the debris cleared. And this Nicols most certainly did, erecting another fine building on the site. However, history has a habit of repeating itself and 33 years later another fire broke out, but this time the fire brigade were better prepared and equipped. This second fire started on the right hand side of the shop due to an electrical fault and quickly spread to the lift shaft. Fortunately there was an immediate response from the Redhill section of the Borough fire brigade and the fire rapidly brought under control.

Though Nicols was prominent because of its location in the town, the early nineteen hundreds was blessed with a large number of very successful companies and businesses. Phillips store close to the Reading Arch Bridge, was as one old resident remarked, " a glory hole store which sold just about everything". And this was true of several other smaller shops, such as Hoares and Sidney Bouchers in Station Road. But it was the variety of stores and shops and the wide range of goods they had to offer, which were the features of Redhill at this time. Businesses which included William Stenning the timber merchant near the station, W.A. Buckland maker of beds and chairs in Grove Hill Road and the busiest shop of them all in the High Street, Joe Chandler the fish merchants. And then there were the pubs; scores of them both grand and dingy, most now gone but not forgotten. Names which reflected the origins of the town, such as the Locomotive in Ladbroke Road, the South Eastern and the Warwick Hotel. Pubs like the Sussex Arms, The Royal Oak and the Britannia, which survived for some years only to succumb in the end to the whims of the developers. Others, even earlier casualties like the Ship and Anchor famous for its mulled porter, pease pudding and faggots, which disappeared in 1912. All gone as have some of the names too, though the pubs survive; the George and Dragon now just plain Dragon, with The Anchor renamed Garlands and reflective perhaps of the new Redhill, The Office, where once The Tower was the name on everyone's lips. And it was here in The Tower that drovers at the day's end, sipped their beers and talked of the cattle they had sold. Cattle they had driven to market down the cobbled alley opposite, known then as "Blood and Guts Street" and now the entrance road to the Marketfield car park. And it was from the windows of The Tower on 18th June 1903, that drinkers watched the young music-hall artiste Mlle. Florence pass by. But not in any orthodox sort of way, for she had accepted a challenge to walk backwards on a large ball from London to Brighton. This remarkable feat she eventually accomplished in five days, arriving in Brighton on 21st June.

And there were other 'happenings' too, though not quite so spectacular.

Nonetheless, the discovery of ancient flints at Arthur Trower's Wiggey estate, were considered an important 'find'. And as similar discoveries had been made on Redstone Hill, it led experts to conclude that Wiggey Lane at one time, was a direct continuation of Frenches Road and used by Neolithic Man four to five thousand years previously. Admittedly it was not headline news for the general public but the arrival in Merstham of two famous stage personalities was a different matter. At least it was, when they were the principal comedian of the day Seymour Hicks and his actress wife Ellaline Terris. Following a number of successful shows in London, they later appeared in J.M. Barrie's play Quality Street at the Vaudeville Theatre. Taking up residence in a house called The Old Forge, their arrival prompted the comment, 'ah now all the quality live here'! As a result the name stuck and the north end of the old High Street, has been known as Quality Street ever since. In 1936 whether by accident or design, Macintosh launched its famous chocolate assortment Quality Street.

Another personality was Henry Gurney who died in 1905. He was a member of the Norfolk family of Quaker Bankers, reputed to have been one of the greatest discount houses in the world during the first half of the nineteenth century. In 1866 the bank went bankrupt with debts of £11 million and Henry Gurney was forced to sell his home Nutfield Priory.

But in the business world there were personalities too, though they tended to be less conspicuous, immersed as they were in the fierce competition that now gripped the town. And the extent of this competition was evident along the entire length of the Brighton Road, with multiple butchers, grocers, bakers and dairies all advertising that their products were the best. Yet most appeared to make a living and have plenty of customers; certainly this was the case with Alfred Knight, for he had a second butchers shop at No. 79 and a third in Merstham. He was representative of the new breed of entrepreneurs who had arrived in Redhill at the turn of the century. Businessmen who were quick to identify the excellent prospects which existed and the need to supply quality products. Not that keeping meat fresh can have been easy, for the only method of refrigeration was an ice box at the back of the shop. But Alfred Knight did and prospered, employing his brother-in-law and several staff to run the three shops. A personality he might not have been, but he was typical of his trade and proud too, donning a bowler hat in the winter and a straw boater during the summer.

The proliferation of business, not just in Redhill but in Reigate too, highlighted the need to form a body to represent the traders. In April 1908 as a result of several informal discussions, the Reigate and Redhill Chamber of Commerce was founded at a meeting held in the Market Hall. A subsequent meeting at Lakers Hotel was attended by fourteen tradesmen, half from each side of the Borough. Commenting on the occasion the Chairman Mr J.R. Clarke concluded;

"It took them pretty well an hour to get into line".

He explained that the Reigate men thought the Redhill men were going too fast for them. However, they "came into line" and, as a result, there was a further meeting at which a memorandum and articles of association were drawn up.

"We have done what we thought was right for the interests of the Borough", claimed Mr Clarke, "and what is good for one side must be good for the other. If the Chamber of Commerce is able to make people believe this, it will at least have done one good thing". It was agreed that co-operation was essential between both areas and that there should be no "great-divide" between traders, as there previously had been in the political arena of the Council.

The new Chamber was enthusiastically welcomed by traders large and small, including the local coach and carriage building firm of Chalmers & Company. They had built the first Royal Mail motor van and, as part of the deal, one of the family had driven it on the first mail run from Dorking to Redhill in 1905. The van had a 20hp engine, solid tyres and with a top speed of 15mph travelling in it must have been extremely uncomfortable for the driver Ian Chalmers. He was not the regular driver, but Chalmers' contract with the Post Office stipulated that they had to supply drivers. However, there were conditions and that the type of driver must be, "competent, steady, honest, sober, careful, who shall not be less than 25 or above 50 years of age and of good character and duly licensed to drive a motor car". But providing a driver was only one of the conditions, as the firm had also to supply him with a uniform, "consisting of a leather cap with dropped peak, bearing the letters G P O in gilt". It was also a requirement to maintain the vehicle, supply oil and petrol and ensure that it kept to its schedule. For all this Chalmers received

£240.7/- a year, payable monthly in instalments.

Cars were still out of the reach of the pocket of the average working man and were generally considered "rich men's toys." Nonetheless, more and more were making their appearance each year and consequently, road surfaces began to deteriorate. However, this problem was recognised at an early stage and by 1910 main roads were almost entirely tarred. With better surfaces, motorists had the inclination to break speed limits and the Brighton Road was an irresistible temptation. Eventually a speed limit was imposed through the town and policemen instructed to ensure it was observed. This was probably unfair, as many of the earlier models travelled considerably slower than horses and carriages. But motorists were far from popular and easy prey for enterprising constables seeking promotion. A fact which was graphically illustrated in Punch Magazine, where a policeman was shown lurking behind a wall ready to pounce on an oncoming motorist. And this certainly happened in 1910 following a number of complaints received by the Head Constable. Complaints which referred to the "nuisances" caused by motor cars in the Borough and the, "rough, noisy and disorderly behaviour of children on the Commons". However, one of these "nuisances" did its best to cancel out the other and nearly succeeded, but for the efforts of PC Barnett. The good officer was commended by the Watch Committee and received a gratuity of 10/6d for,

"his diligence in saving a boy from being run over by a motor car".

By 1912 the volume of motor traffic had reached around 200 a day just south of Redhill, with much of it comprising of heavy lorries and buses. This daily wear and tear cut up the "improved" road surfaces so badly, that experiments were made with tarmacadam on the busiest roads in the country and these proved to be effective. And this was good news for the East Surrey Traction Company, who had begun their first regular service from Redhill to Merstham the previous year using a Leyland motor bus. Good news too for passengers travelling between Redhill and Reigate in the cramped single-deck buses. But each of them did have an extra seat in the front beside the driver, from where the fare was paid to the conductor through a small window.

To accommodate the demand for public road transport, it was not long before the East Surrey Traction Company introduced open-topped double-deckers on most of their routes. And one of the first ran from Redhill, down Hooley Lane and along Victoria Road, before grinding its way through

Earlswood and on to Horley. The late Arthur King remembered it as a
> "bus that had solid tyres and hard seats.
> Open to the skies it was, making you
> duck your head when going under railway
> bridges. Wet and all, but they did
> supply waterproof sheets".

Inconvenient perhaps, but these pioneering bus passengers were a hardy breed. And well they needed to be, particularly when they were obliged to alight from buses at the bottom of Redstone Hill and walk up. This was necessary when there was snow and ice, though not uncommon at other times when engines had a tendency to overheat when overloaded. And this frequently occurred on race days, when enormous charabancs struggled up the numerous hills to Epsom. But there were occasions when help was at hand, or perhaps more aptly put, young lads with an eye for business. For them, earning extra pennies was vital and the long, steep hill which in those days stretched past the Sewage Farm, the hunting ground. As the heavily-laden charabancs gradually slowed down to a crawl, scores of youngsters would dash out and help the struggling vehicles up the last yards of the hill. As a reward some of the passengers who had remained on board would throw out pennies, which the lads gratefully gathered up. As Horace Cornish remembers;

> "The bobbies didn't like it and would chase us and give us a clout, if they
> could catch us. But that didn't happen often".

Though the volume of traffic was now quite considerable on the main roads, the peace of St. Johns remained relatively undisturbed apart from "the comings and goings" around the Workhouse. But even these went generally unnoticed by the local residents. True the Workhouse with its high walls and bleak buildings was a grim presence, but even this harshness was softened by its woodland setting. A setting that was once described as, "affording one of the finest views taking in the vast expanse of the Weald to the south".

Referring to the former Workhouse, H.E. Green in his book The Surrey Hills remarked;

> "I have my eye on the Workhouse there, when the time comes
> when my books are no longer read, and I have to take my
> share of that fund to which I have been contributing
> through the rate-collector for so many years. I think the

rooms at the Redhill Workhouse should be reserved for broken-down poets, painters and descriptive writers".

And a short distance away another thriving, self-supporting community also remained undisturbed. Thriving, because in Earlswood small shops had sprung up to cater for the villagers and the growing population to the east of the railway line. Life was relaxed and peaceful. Little had changed here; Edwardian England had become Georgian England, but the shadow of a Victorian way of life still remained. There were of course exceptions such as the occasional motor car, which swept through the village in a cloud of dust. But it had no sooner arrived than it had departed; noisy, backfiring and chased by a group of village lads. For this was fun and a break from routine, as were the very exceptional visits to town to see the "moving picture" shows. And these could be seen at the Cinema Royal and Family Theatre in Station Road, on the site of the present Arcade. Later known as The Picture House, the cinema was the first picture theatre in the Borough and opened for business in October 1909. It cost just 3d admission and patrons were assured, that the seating arrangements for 350 people would "leave nothing to be desired". In the local press it was announced that;

"The Electric Picture Palace Co. are now showing all the Most Recent and up-to-date living and animated Creations: Comedy, Drama, Trajedy, Farce: Instructive, Comic and Amusing Pictures".

But the sands of time were running out for "amusing picture shows", or quiet evening walks past the recently renamed Reigate and Redhill Hospital on White Post Hill. For the ominous clouds of war were gathering, as billboards beckoned young men and old to arms. Huge billboards that invited them to serve their country. Posters pasted on walls and doors with precise instructions. Report to the recruiting office in Ladbroke Road or assemble at the Market Hall on certain nights. And they did, these young men and old of Redhill; emerging from the terraced blocks of Monson Road and Hooley; from palatial residences and modest cottages, united in the common bond to serve their country. Railwaymen, farmers and gentlemen too, joined by a scoutmaster from the Earlswood (2nd Reigate Troop). And off to war they marched through the streets of the town they loved; marching to the sounds of pipes and drums and a thousand cheering voices; sounds to remember in the sludge and blood of Ypres, the Somme and a hundred other battlefields; memories to hold on to and help them through the agony and hell that was the Great War.

But for youngsters the Great War was older people's business, like the horses;

> "During the '14-18 war, I remember when they came down to Earlswood and got the horses. They used to go around and collect them from the farms and the Common. And they packed them in the trains. Then some of these horses fell down and couldn't get up again and used to get trod to death".

For the fire brigade 1914 was a memorable year with the delivery of their first motorised engine, a Dennis escape tender. This was a vast improvement both technically and by the speed firemen could reach the scene of a call out. Certainly this was demonstrated in December 1915, when a fire destroyed Love and Malcolmson's Athenaeum Printing Works in Brighton Road. Part of the works dated from 1869 and at one time the Surrey Mirror had been printed there. The fire was apparently a large one, as fire crews from Redhill, Reigate, Meadvale, South Park and Earlswood were called out. But due to their efficiency, all 140 staff escaped without death or serious injury by using the outside staircases and ladders. The Dennis tender was again in action in 1917, when a munitions train full of live shells and fuses, was found to be alight at Redhill station. The brigade, which consisted at the time of "willing but rather ineffectual auxiliaries" was quickly on the scene. However, despite their inexperience, the blazing trucks of shells were segregated from the rest of the train and the flames extinguished before they exploded.

Throughout the years of war, there was a steady stream of munitions and troop trains through Redhill. Troops were also stationed in the town with three regiments billetted on Earlswood Common, opposite Somerset Road and Clarence Walk in Meadvale. Here village shops benefited from the unexpected trade, though many felt they had been "invaded". But there was no real invasion or bombings from the skies. Only the reminder of war as the blackout continued and the deaths of local men were reported in the papers. Reports like the one in 1915 which sadly announced that "two of Redhill's sons gave their lives in action, performing heroic deeds". Heroic deeds which posthumously earned them each the Victoria Cross.

With the war continuing year after year and no end in sight, the resulting drain on manpower was quite significant. Men from all walks of life and of all ages were being called up, as the appalling losses on the battlefields mounted. And this left shortages of manpower in a variety of jobs including the farming industry. Now it was necessary to fill the gaps with child labour and as a consequence, education was seriously disrupted. However, for the children it was a welcome change from boring lessons, as schools were encouraged to grow vegetables, potatoes and other crops. And this was work they enjoyed, particularly picking blackberries for jam and helping their mothers knit socks for soldiers. A united effort that united families and joined strangers in friendship. For these were unusual times never experienced before, although for most in Redhill life continued as usual. Certainly the Redhill Society of Instrumentalists did, performing regularly to packed houses in the Market Hall Rooms. But on one occasion in 1916 when they gave a special performance, they announced in their programme that it would be held on the night of the full moon. This was to "enable everyone to get home in the blackout". On another night the Society arranged with the South Eastern Railway to hold the last train, as the concert was due to end half an hour after the scheduled departure time.

There was relief and joy when the war ended, though perhaps muted by the appalling losses of England's young manhood. Hardly a family in the land was unaffected, for almost all had suffered a loss or welcomed home a wounded relative. The relief was for the end of bloodshed and the hope of many peaceful years ahead. In Redhill as in other towns throughout the land, street parties were organised to celebrate. Pianos were wheeled out and long tables set up, decorated with bunting and laden with food and drinks. Overhead and across the streets more bunting and flags stretched as far as the eyes could see. Peace had come at last, but at a terrible cost.

Looking down Earlswood Road towards the Station Hotel, later to become the Chestnut Public House. Though the picture was taken around 1910, this view remains virtually unchanged today.

The Market Hall in 1910 (courtesy E.Freeman)

The High Street in 1905 looking towards the Wheatsheaf in the distance on the left. None of the shops survive. Jones and Jennings went out of business in the 1990s. (courtesy E. Freeman)

Nat. Tel. 395.

M_____ 191_

Bought of A. Knight,

Family Butcher.

FAMILIES WAITED ON DAILY FOR ORDERS.

DAIRY-FED PORK.

PICKLED TONGUES.

79 & 139 BRIGHTON ROAD, REDHILL.

The Nicol's Department Store fire soon after it had started. Two jets are at work, one protecting the Wheatsheaf Public House. (courtesy Reigate Priory Museum)

MESSRS NICOL & SON'S PREMISES. 1901.

Nicol's Department Store before it was destroyed by fire on 25 May 1901. The fire started in the corsetry window behind the street lamp.
(courtesy Reigate Priory Museum)

The scene on Whit Sunday 26 May 1901 (courtesy Reigate Priory Museum)

Local "Fat Stock Show" display, outside the butcher's shop of Alfred Knight at 139, Brighton Road, in the early 1900s.
(courtesy Margaret Knight)

London Road looking towards the Crossroads in the early 1900s. (courtesy E. Freeman)

FRENCHES ROAD/LONDON ROAD, ST. JOSEPH'S CONVENT IN BACKGROUND

(courtesy E. Freeman)

READING ARCH c1900, LOOKING TOWARDS TOWN CENTRE

(courtesy E. Freeman)

Chapter 8
LAUGHTER AND TEARS

As peace returned to Redhill, it was apparent that the Great War had changed a way of life; a way of life that even through those grim years had not entirely shrugged off the Victorian mentality. But the Great War changed all that and one of the principal reasons was the emancipation of women. Another was that the great divide between the classes had narrowed, at least in outlook if not in wealth. 1920 was a time for hope and the prospect of better living conditions; a time for new fashions, new attitudes and, of course, the Charleston; above all it was a time for youth.

But some things never change; like the family ritual of church on Sunday, a good dinner and then an early evening walk across the fields. Memories that are still vivid over seventy years later.

> "On Sundays we used to walk round, me mum and dad and us, by the lakes, through the copse and over to the Beehive pub at Dovers. Used to stop there for a lemonade. Of course I used to have lemonade in them days and me dad had the beer. Cost tuppence with a pickled onion and a lump of cheese. Then we'd walk along to the Angel at Woodhatch and go through Hayward's farm. It was all meadow and cultivated then. Used to go up a little old sand path and climb over a stile and come to the Ship. We'd have another lemonade there. Then we used to go as far as another pub on the way back. The Flying Scud it was; and me and me mother and another lady would go into a little bar, the Bottle and Jug it was called, and we'd have another lemonade out the front. Afterwards we'd go over to me grandpa's cottage near the church. I always remember him living there, because he had one of those old grandfather clocks. And we young ones would sit there for hours just pulling the chains. I always remember those Sundays. Used to be great. Used to be marvellous walking through

the fields and the copse, seeing rabbits and squirrels
and a fox now and again".

The fields through which the young lad and his family strolled have now vanished. The large estates of Woodhatch and Meadvale cover the land that was once lush and green. It was here in Meadvale in the early twenties that he and his friends helped the farmer with his hay making.

"And that's where I first sampled cider. Cor! and
it was cider and all! Used to be what they'd made
on the farm".

Happy memories of youth; carefree days that were sometimes hard but rarely dull, filled with adventure and daring. Days that brought Horace Cornish rich rewards scouring the dump near Emelyn Road, which was used by Woolworth's lorries for their rubbish.

"We used to go along and find all sorts
of things, even halfpennies".

And halfpennies and pennies were like gold dust for little boys, especially when poverty was never far away and pocket money merely dreamt about. For a penny or two would buy an assortment of sweets that would last a week, or for Horace's dad, a pint at the Station Hotel.

"You could get a bit of bread and cheese in the
pub for a penny. Many a time me old man would
bring that out to me. Five Woodbine fags cost
a penny in them days".

Days when money seemed to go further and businesses survive on narrow profit margins. Businesses and shops that were largely family orientated in the early twenties and many of them newly opened. Shops squeezed into every available space the length of Brighton Road to the very doorstep of the New Inn. In fact it was said that there were more diverse businesses in this one road, than there were in the whole of Redhill. For a gentle stroll from the Reading Arch Bridge up the right hand side of Brighton Road, brought shoppers past the Anchor pub on the corner and then a multitude of small shops. Many established since the turn of the century, but now added to by ex-soldiers trying to make a living. Further up there was a church, the Athenaeum Printing Works, a garage, cycle shop and then Denny the milkman's yard, now occupied by Country Plant Hire. It was a common sight to see him drive his cattle across the main road, down Brook Road and then along Hooley Lane towards Redstone Hollow. Where today there is a housing estate, in the twenties there was open pasture and it was here that old Denny grazed his cows. Next to the New Inn one of Redhill's most popular bakers had premises, in addition to their shop in the High Street.

And a feature in advertising at this time was the status symbol of a van that would deliver. But then everyone knew that Lawrence & Sons in Cromwell Road had the most modern removal vans in the business. What they did not know however, was that the business was literally 'poetry in motion'.

"Our reputation stands supreme,
our men are skilled and very keen,
Removals done in perfect style,
and that is why our Patrons smile
and say 'we can't be beaten'.
Our terms are moderate and fair
we move your furniture anywhere,
From door to door or into store
without it getting broken.
Our vans are of the latest make,
our testimonials they are great,
So see that you make no mistake
if you should be removing".

Though Brighton Road, the High Street and all the other shopping areas were bustle and activity most days of the week, Marketfield on a Saturday still held "centre stage". It was probably the most popular market for miles around, packed with gaily-decorated stalls selling vegetables, fruit, meat, clothes, pots and pans and of course sweets for the children. Every variety imaginable, from penny humbugs to long stringy liquorice and gob-stoppers. And these were the stalls Eddie Waller remembers, as well as the pungent smell of the flares which lit them.

"The sweet stalls were open to the elements, not
wrapped or anything like that. There was also the
'cure all' man, who seemed to have a pill to remedy
every known illness. There was also a man who sold
boot polish or a sort of paint, that shone shoes as

> good as new. He would clean somebody's boots free
> as a sales gimmick, but wouldn't do any more free
> until he had sold a good few tins of this stuff.
> Then there was the man who had a suitcase full of
> packets. These he would hold up and say, 'here's
> one, here's two, give me sixpence'. And of course
> nobody would. So he'd open a packet and there was
> a watch. Of course this had the effect of drawing
> the crowd in, but they never did get a watch! I
> think he was sleight of hand. It was a great market
> then; full of excitement for youngsters".

And indeed it was a great day out for youngsters; to wander around the stalls and only spend their pennies when they had found the best buys; to wait with growing excitement as the winter dusk descended and the flickering lamps of the stalls were lit. And then home to a supper of bargain meat that mother had bought; tired but happy. Home for Eddie Waller was Shrewsbury Road, from where he and his brother Cyril would walk to school at St. Joseph's in Chapel Road. And it was from here that he was the first boy to be entered with a scholarship to Reigate Grammar School. It was also another "first", as it was considered at the time that Catholic boys should not be sent to the Grammar School. However, despite being an "outsider and very scared because of the large number of boys, I soon adjusted to life there".

For S.A. Field school was the Southern Provincial Police School off London Road, which he attended from 1925 until 1939. Soon after the First World War ended the school expanded and in 1923, the imposing mansion of "Frenches" was acquired and became the main school building. Founded in 1890 by Catherine Gurney, the establishment catered for orphans and the fatherless children of policemen. The residential part of the school was housed in "Woodlands" (now the site of the East Surrey College) and the whole complex included meadows, woods and orchards. In 1949 the school was taken over by Surrey County Council and became St. Nicholas's. But for young Field the orphanage school was a happy place.

> "I was there as a pupil for 14 years, where I
> received an excellent character-building, if
> old-fashioned education, for which I shall be

eternally grateful".

A beautiful place, with fine old buildings and picturesque gardens long since demolished; ploughed up and buried beneath the foundations of several hundred homes. A beautiful place which the Merstham schoolmaster Vicars-Bell obviously overlooked, when commenting on the state of Redhill in 1921.

> "I think I owe the fact that I have lived all my adult
> life in villages, to the fact that Redhill was a horrid
> little town in which my childhood was spent. Almost
> twenty miles from London and on the main Brighton Road,
> it never seemed to offer any reason for its existence,
> nor to have any ancient traditions, nor to contain any
> buildings of dignity and beauty. I rather fancy it must
> have sprung up in the years of the great railway boom.
> A crossroads provided an excuse for a hideous market
> hall (I could never discover that it had any connection
> with a market), a bank which looked like a wing of
> Dartmoor Prison, a granite-faced public house and a
> large drapers store, in which customers' change went
> whizzing through the air on shining wires. There were
> two streets of mediocre shops and then rows and rows
> and rows of mean houses interspersed with little
> shops which sold newspapers, cheap sweets, paraffin
> and tea. All this lay huddled in a marshy basin, but
> on the upper rim of this circular conglomeration
> there were quiet roads of large houses".

Harsh words indeed and not very complimentary. But many of the "mean houses" and "little shops", were the original buildings of the early development and by the early twenties must have been drab and decaying. But not so the Shrewsbury Road that Eddie Waller remembers or the Cottage Hospital, which in 1923 was renamed the East Surrey.

> "It was a grand occasion the opening of the hospital extension
> by Princess Astrid. That extension was the one facing the Common.
> I remember standing there with my aunt Mabel who used to come
> down from Cambridge. She was great fun and I remember her turning
> to me and saying, 'we're going to see Princess ASTRIDE'"!

Aunt Mabel was a character and so were several others who lived locally;

> "The house next to the Cottage Hospital belonged to Mr Grimes who ran the Pavilion Cinema, on the corner of Chapel Road and the High Street. 'The Fleapit' it used to be called. We used to go there quite often. And when the lights went out before the film, there was a great rustling noise as everyone moved from the twopenny seats to the fourpenny! I always remember him, because he had one of those beautiful French cars with a round front. My father had one of the first cars in the road, a Morris, which he used for his work as a commercial traveller for Lever Brothers.
>
> Among our neighbours was Mr Lilley who had the butchers shop at Reffell's Bridge and a Mr Boniface. I remember his name to this day, for he had two rosy cheeks".

And then there were the "visiting characters" who called at homes offering their services. The Knife Grinder, Cat's Meat Man, Chair Repairs Man and of course the Rag and Bone Man. All characters, as was the old man with the horse and cart loaded with coal, that slowly climbed the steep incline of Hooley Lane from the railway sidings. And then across the Brighton Road and a stop to allow his horse a drink at the water trough, which then stood outside The Firs in Mill Street. After a rest another steep climb up Mill Street to the top opposite Linkfield Street. And here was a favourite drinking trough, self-filling with the water and moisture that ran off the Common. As Eddie Waller remarks;

> "Horses were not forgotten in those days. In fact there was yet another water trough at Shaw's Corner and most of them had to be filled every day. Shaw's Corner was very picturesque in the twenties with a beautiful chestnut tree, surrounded by circular seats. Unfortunately it was cut down when the site was chosen for the Borough War Memorial. There was alot of controvery over it at the time, particularly as to why

it was facing the Forester's Arms and neither Reigate or Redhill".

The general strike of 1926 and the depression which followed, brought bankruptcies, hardship and despair across the nation. In Redhill people clamoured for jobs but opportunities were few. The employers of one local company took on those applicants who quoted only the lowest pay they would accept. It could hardly have been termed a living wage, but it was work. With widespread redundancies throughout the country as the depression hit hard, the poorer sections of the community were the first to suffer. Deprived of work they were unable to pay rents and were promptly and viciously evicted from their homes. In Redhill many were sent to 'Doss Houses' or the Workhouse, where men were separated from their wives and children. It was to split many families asunder, but the authorities felt they had done the best they could.

Poverty was now closer than ever for many families desperately clinging to their homes; and the pennies and halfpennies they earned took on a new meaning. But they were few and far between, difficult to earn, though Charlewood's Dairy in Earlswood and Denny's did offer youngsters occasional work, mucking out the stables or the cowsheds. For this work they could earn as much as twopence. And rubbing down a horse often brought a reward of a fresh cup of milk, which was more than welcome for lads with empty tummies. In fact any job was seized upon by Redhill's youngsters, whether it was caddying on the golf course or delivering newspapers. But they also had time for fun and, despite the hardships, Horace Cornish remembers a community of life and laughter; of donkeys and carts and playing darts against a wooden fence. Entertainment for youngsters was what they made themselves. Televisions were yet to be invented; radios were for the rich; there was little money. The streets became the playing grounds.

> "We used to play marbles up against the wall of the old corner shop and make a hole in the wall. You'd have half a dozen marbles and the one who got most in the hole, got the lot. These were the things we did in them days. Of a night we used to play around the old lamp post until the old woman called you to go in. They was all gas lamps then. An old fellow used to come around on a bike and light them. Conkers

> was another thing, playin' with the old conkers. You
> don't see much of that these days. Life was tough then.
> To get grub you'd have to go and earn it. Bread and
> dripping; I used to love a bit of bread and dripping
> I did. We was poor then. I remember going to school
> then with hardly any decent shoes on me feet".

For Mrs L. Gardiner who was born in 1912, the Depression was a nightmare, but she was fortunate to have a job even if it did not pay much money. She stayed for many years in a

> "very rough lodging-house at the bottom of Grove Road.
> We lived with my granddad and he and my uncle worked
> at the Tanyard. Money wasn't much then, just five shillings
> a week when I was fourteen. Gave my mum four and kept
> one for clothes; couldn't give her less as my dad died in
> 1923 when he was 42. He worked for Stonemans
> when it was horses. He used to be on the first carriage
> behind the hearse".

Mrs Gardiner also remembers the twenties as happy days, despite the hardship and poverty of the depression years. Fun was what children created themselves; swinging from a rope tied to the arms of a lamp post by rugged string, or chanting songs and jumping over skipping ropes tied to drainpipes. A toy was a treasured possession, especially the doll made from castoffs and stuffed with old newspapers.

For many people the luxury of electricity was non-existent. Paraffin and gas lamps were the norm and families were considered "lucky" if there was a street lamp outside the front window. After all it was free and usually sufficient to provide enough light in the room. But for young children it was eerie; hardly daring to look towards the dark corners of the room.

> "It was cold in those terraces, mostly damp with cardboard-
> like walls. You could hear the neighbours very clearly day
> and night, but mostly in the late dark nights because of
> the silence. Talking of silence, evenings for us kids were
> very lonely in the winter months when bad weather kept us
> indoors. I would hear the clock ticking loudly in the
> shadows of that small room, where it became very depressed.

> A small candle to see us up the stairs was all we were
> allowed. We never used the outside 'lavs', just a chamber
> or 'poe' as we called it".

But some children did or were made to go, "out the back to the small shed". During dark, wet winter nights, this usually was a journey dreaded by young children. Though they always had a hurricane lamp and a hovering parent to keep the 'bogeyman' away, it was nonetheless a daunting experience.

> "You'd sit there on the cold, damp wooden seat
> with the lamp in the half-open doorway to give
> light. You knew your mum or dad was outside and
> you were safe, but it was the flickering of the
> lamp that was scary. The light catching the
> black cobwebs that kept moving in the wind. That
> was the worst".

The passing years may have faded some memories of those days almost seventy years ago. But for another Grove Road resident, the memories of happy days and empty stomachs will never fade.

> "Looking back on those days as children, we were happy
> most times having nothing, but grown-ups never had
> peace, at least not until things improved and most
> folk waited a long time for that".

And they most certainly did as the Depression dragged on with little prospect of improvement in sight. Survival was foremost in most people's minds and food the priority. At the grocers loose broken biscuits could be bought for a few pence and even wholesome biscuit crumbs were snapped up. Sweetshops sold "dusty allsorts", which were the remains at the bottoms of sweet jars before they were re-stocked. While the greengrocer sold his "slightly pecked fruit" at a discount, early customers at the bakery could take advantage of "yesterday's bread and stale cakes". But for many the Sunday joint was just a memory of better times; to be seen at the butchers, but not eaten on the dinner tables of Grove Road. Rather it was,

> "sixpence worth of cuttings, which were the
> trimmings from the joints of meat. When
> cut up with a pennyworth of mixed veg and
> an Oxo cube added, it would make a nourishing

pot of stew".

Life could only get better and this it gradually did as the twenties gave way to the thirties. The Depression had dominated most people's lives and over-shadowed events, but the expansion of the town had continued. And so had the Borough Council, with added responsibilities such as the upkeep of the Commons, which had finally been transferred to them in perpetuity by the Lord of the Manor, Henry Somers Somerset. All of the founding fathers of the early businesses had now passed on, but sons and grandsons continued to build upon the firm foundations that had been set. Businesses such as Halls, Bucklands, Jennings, Stonemans and many more. And it was this expansion of trade and the gradual return to better times, that brought about a very noticeable increase in road traffic. This of course presented policing problems.

In 1930 James Metcalfe retired as Head Constable after thirty six years service and was succeeded by William Beacher. It was effectively the end of an era of old policing methods that had covered the transition from horses and carriages to motor cars. But the efficiency of the police had improved immensely during his time, due in no small measure to his reputation as a disciplinarian. Perhaps this had been taken a bit too far on one occasion when he issued instructions that there was to be, ' a quarter of an hour's drill in saluting by numbers each day, until the Head Constable is satisfied'.

With the arrival of William Beacher and traffic a major problem to tackle, the Borough Watch Committee were pressured into purchasing two 500cc 'Red Wing' Panthers. This was the birth of the mobile section, or the 'Courtesy Cops' as they came to be known and added new depth to police operations. As former police constable R.C. Brownlow, one of the original mobile cops recalled some years later;

> "I well remember our initial briefing;the West Sussex cops were held up as an example, but despite this the Mayor immediately christened us 'Burke and Hare', after the famous old time body snatchers. My colleague as a 'Courtesy Cop' was 'Burke' Jock Mason".

William 'Jock' Mason had joined the Borough Police in 1926 having arrived in Redhill from Scotland. Formerly a mechanic, he was eager to volunteer for mobile duties and could hardly contain his excitement, as the machines were prepared and instructions issued. Now mobile on his new Panther, 'Jock' was soon in action. As he waited near the Reading Arch Bridge, he noticed a car being driven at speed down the Brighton Road. It overtook three cars as it approached the Market Hall and he estimated it was travelling about 33 mph. Since the speed limit in the town was 10mph, he gave chase. The car continued northwards at the same speed, overtaking a bus and then another car. Having exceeded 40mph approaching Gatton Point, Mason managed to stop the driver. At the court case some weeks later the magistrates were told;

"After Frenches it passed several cars on the offside of the road, practically all the way to Gatton Point. When stopped, defendant said that he had come up the hill in third gear. When told he would be reported, he replied that he would report the constable. He maintained that the car could not go fast, and that the only cars he passed were going the other way.(laughter)".

Taking a break from his Panther duties soon afterwards, Jock Mason spotted a couple of men loitering near the Royal Oak in the High Street. As one of the men was carrying an attache case he became suspicious and questioned them. They replied they were "down from London for the day looking for work". Jock decided to take them to Redhill police station and have a look at the attache case. It was a wise decision, for inside he found an assortment of articles which included 2 sheath knives, one jack knife, 2 pairs of pliers, a chisel and a revolver.

But foot patrolling was not Jock's scene and he could hardly wait until he was gripping the handlebars of his Panther again. Though most drivers when arrested for dangerous driving "came quietly", there were a few who reacted differently. One such man became quite aggressive when Jock arrested him in October 1932 for drunken driving in The Cutting. After being subdued and brought to the police station, he admitted having consumed several pints and added;

"but for God's sake, don't make a case of it".

He then made several rambling statements.

"I am entirely in your hands. I shall give up

cars and the other. I simply swerved across the
road, because I was talking to the other man
sitting in the car beside me".

This convinced Mason the man was quite definitely drunk as;
"....there was no person sitting beside him in the
car when I stopped him. In fact there were no other
persons in the car at all except the driver".

When formally charged the man told Mason and his colleagues;
"I am beginning to like you"!

Jock Mason remembers "The Grange" on the Frenches estate, where he lived with his family in one of the converted stables. In particular he remembers the big pond and the graceful swans that swam in it.

But the days of graceful living were fast coming to an end and the conversion of mansions like "The Grange" into separate residences, was a sign of the times. For others the fate was demolition, which was what happened to Wiggey when the estate was sold in 1938. In many ways this was a tragedy, for the beautiful gardens and daffodil fields had given pleasure to visitors for many years. And this was true of Gatton too, where Sir Jeremiah Colman of mustard fame threw open his grounds for firework displays. He had an absolute passion for fireworks and many spectacular displays were held, the most memorable being a "special one" for the coronation of George VI and Queen Elizabeth. The centrepiece was a giant portrait of the King and Queen and enormous crowds from Redhill attended, including one small boy who found the fireworks,

"were so bright that you couldn't see after they
were over. It was a wonder there wasn't an accident
involving someone losing their footing and getting
trampled - for there was a mass stampede to get off
the estate and home.
They were great displays, but they came to an end
when the old mansion burnt down and many valuable
paintings and other works of art were destroyed".

Another young boy who attended the displays was S.E. Tribe, but he usually had to be up early in the mornings. Delivering newspapers is still very much part of early morning Redhill life and the routine just the same as it was in 1932. For young Tribe the princely sum of 2/6d a week was good money, even though it meant reporting early to Shepherds in the High Street each morning. But once on his round, he joined the other paper boys in the ritual "dawn chorus".

> "Once on the rounds we would whistle the popular tunes of the day, as we met up with other paper boys from other newsagents, all whistling. The postman, milkman and bakers would join in. It would all die down as we moved away".

Delivering papers to the large houses was always fun, as most had long halls and highly polished floors.

> "What we used to do when putting the paper through the letter box, was to hit it with the palm of the hand. The idea was to send it whizzing as far as possible. In any event it probably saved the maid a few steps on the slippery floor".

Then young Tribe would return to Shepherds for another batch and pass the milkmen, still whistling. He knew most of them well, including the man from Dennys in Brighton Road.

> "Of course they were all horses and carts then, something like chariots with two large wheels. There were churns filled with milk at the front, with a tap which would draw off a full bucket. The milkman would ladle it into containers to deliver, or take a pail to the houses where housewives would be waiting with jugs. This was all before the bottles came along".

There was no noticeable increase in the pace of life during the thirties, but the whole period from the Great War to the Second World War has often been described as the "false summer of peace". There was, if anything, a lethargic approach to life; a disbelief that anything could disrupt this peace; a peace that had been so dearly bought with the blood of England's sons, in "the war to end all wars". But not all life was lethargic, far from it. In 1932 the main line between Reigate, Redhill and London was electrified and major alterations made to the station; the fire brigade proudly opened their new station in London Road and announced it could accommodate two engines and an ambulance; while the Borough Council informed the public that Redstone Cemetery was now open for burials. In the sporting world, the year saw the formation of the Redhill and Reigate Athletic Club, following a meeting by a dozen local sportsmen in the Locomotive pub. And athletics were again in the news the following year, when the Borough Police tug-of-war eight won the Surrey County Championships. But new jobs were the main news in 1934, when the Standard Brick and Sand Company began operations, to be soon followed in December when Redhill Aerodrome opened. Designed to accommodate British Air Transport and its subsidiary The Redhill Flying Club, the aerodrome later underwent a series of extensions, which included the erection of a control tower and hangars in 1937. This coincided with the opening of No. 13 Elementary and Reserve Flying Training School. By the outbreak of war, the school was operating 29 Miles Magisters, 6 Tiger Moths, 19 Hart Variants, 4 Battles and 3 Ansons. And coupled with this achievement, was the reputation The Redhill Flying Club had earned as one of the leading clubs in the South of England.

A good reputation had also been earned by the Philanthropic School, which continued its excellent record of rehabilitation, education and training. The school catered for a number of "bad boys", but apart from discipline, most learnt worthwhile trades which they later put to good use in the outside world. In 1938 one of these "bad boys" offered his services to the Warden, Rev R.P.McAuliffe, who was having a problem opening his safe.

"There was a knock on the door and in walked one of my nippers. He said he had heard a rumour that I was having trouble with a locked safe. He would crack it in a jiffy.
'With what?'
'With these sir', he said, extending his ten fingers. 'I knows how sir.' "

Another institution in the news that year was the Workhouse. The abolition of the Poor Law Unions and their Guardians in 1930 meant the transfer of workhouses to the county councils. This included the Workhouse at Earlswood. However, the process of breaking-up the Poor Law institutions took some time, but by 1938 there were almost no able bodied inmates in the workhouses. Unfortunately lack of funds prevented more humane provision for the old and infirm, though by the end of the decade beds in general hospitals were being set aside in "geriatric wards". New hospitals were built or re-designed and the old Workhouse became Redhill General Hospital. About the same time the East Surrey Hospital was enlarged, to cater for a wider geographical area. And with the establishment of the new general hospital, Union Road was renamed Pendleton Road.

It had been a year of steady development and quiet achievement, punctuated by ominous reports of Adolf Hitler's activities on the Continent. And as if to emphasise these "signs of cold comfort", the weather obliged on Christmas morning, by covering Redhill with half a foot of snow. It brought back memories of 1927, but on that occasion there had been blizzards and over ten feet of snow on Reigate Hill.

During the summer of 1939, the Surrey Mirror advertised a 'nice restful voyage to South Africa' for a mere Ü40. But most people could only afford the seaside resorts and, in any case, with Smiths Crisps at 2d and twenty Players Navy Cut at 11d, life was not too bad. At least not quite yet, as the last "false summer of peace" passed quietly towards autumn. It was difficult to convince most people that before very long high explosive bombs would rain down from the skies above Redhill, despite Mr Chamberlain's assurances of "peace in our time".

Once again the young men of Redhill would be called upon to serve their country. And among them Horace Cornish, Arthur King, Jock Mason and a host of others. For Arthur King, the village lad who was now a man, there was no doubt in his mind that war changed everything. Perhaps in particular it was the quality of life that changed more than anything else.

But now as September dawned, the storm-clouds of war were gathering across the English Channel; all too soon, their shadows would cross the fields of Surrey and the years of laughter and tears, would be but memories.

Courtesy Cop.
Jock Mason on his Red Wing Panther 500cc motorbike in 1930. He and R.C.Brownlow were the first 'mobile cops' in Redhill.

The Big Pond and meadows at Frenches in 1930. The pond was later filled in, trees cut down and The Grange in the distance demolished. Today this once peaceful scene has been transformed beyond recognition.(courtesy Jock Mason)

The Cattle Market in 1915 (courtesy E.Freeman)

Brighton Road with Brook Road on the left, many years before it was widened. (courtesy E.Freeman)

"The Knob", Common Road, Earlswood in the summer of 1916.

THE BREAD YOU EAT.

Has a direct effect on your health—If you eat bread that is poorly baked and imperfectly kneaded—bread that is rough and heavy—your health will suffer, and depression will follow—but if you eat bread that is properly prepared—*Grice's Bread*—your health and spirits will benefit. *Grice's Bread* lightens life! Post a card—our van will call.

. . GRICE'S . .
High Street and Brighton Road.

Crash! The car that ended up in the shop window of Hoares next to Lloyds Bank in Station Road. Jack Sales took the photo when working for the Surrey Mirror in 1925.

Earning pennies. Arthur King delivering bread to a lady at Maple Cottages, South Earlswood in 1926.

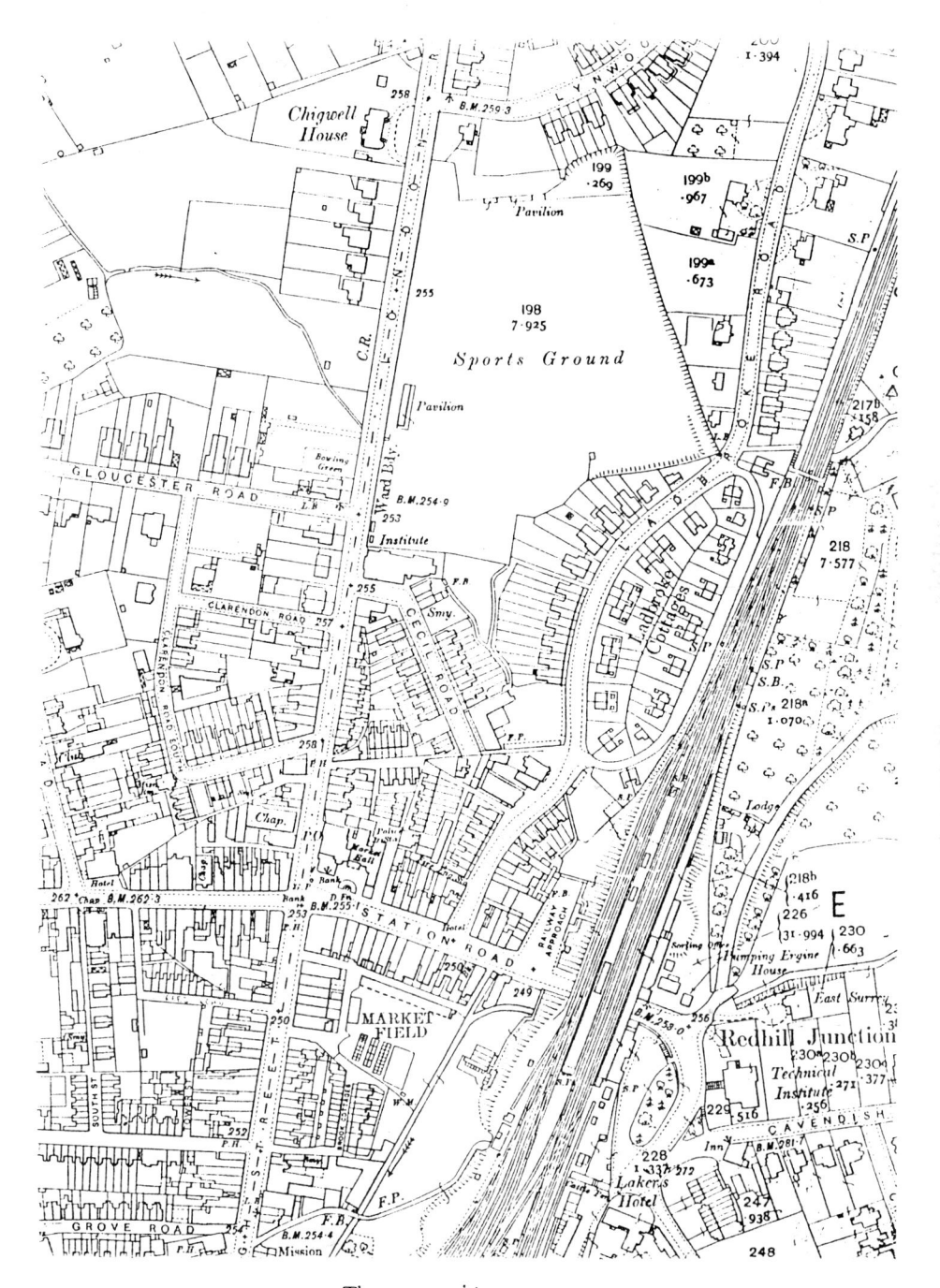

The way it was.
The Town Centre circa 1915

"Frenches"

Boat trips at Earlswood in the 1920s
(courtesy E. Freeman)

Chapter 9
NO SANCTUARY FROM ABOVE

The announcement that Britain was at war with Germany was accepted calmly, stoically almost. Preparations which had been planned for such an eventuality were now put into effect. Many were unobtrusive; behind-the-scene activities but vital for the defence and smooth running of a country at war. These involved organisation of town defences, ensuring that essential services were maintained at all times and properly co-ordinated. From the beginning a blackout was enforced. Black curtains covering windows at night and air raid wardens constantly checking for the slightest chink of light. It was also part of their duties to know everyone in their areas for security reasons and most households co-operated. But on one occasion a warden had to report;

"Blackout very bad. We were met with rudeness and were sworn at. Matter dealt with by police".

This was an exceptional case, as many households checked their own houses themselves and saved wardens valuable time. This was also true of a number of individuals who found themselves on late night shifts. And one of these "unsung" heroines was the East Surrey Hospital's senior cleaner, Mrs Batt. For throughout the war she acted by self-appointment as blackout warden. Each night she saw to it personally that every one of the numerous windows in the building was covered. And, if this was not enough, she checked that all the "prescribed air raid precautions" had been put into practice. It was an "esprit de corps" which would be shown on many occasions; an integral part of the bond that grew between people as the war progressed.

In Redhill carefully prepared plans were soon put into effect under the direction of the Town Council. Their principal business was with civil defence and three members including the Mayor, formed the Emergency Committee which acted as the Council. Their specific duties were to adapt regional directives to meet local conditions. Ordinary day-to-day business was carried out by a committee consisting of chairmen from various Borough committees. It was an arrangement which was to continue throughout the war, as no local elections could be held.

Outwardly at least, associations and individuals carried on normally but so grave seemed the national situation, that the annual carnival was cancelled. As more and more people were drawn into essential services work, there were more obvious signs that Redhill itself might soon be at war. Outdoor lighting in the roads and streets was withdrawn and the 10am postal service cancelled. The drinking fountain outside the Market Hall was removed and an air raid wardens' shelter erected. Other shelters were constructed throughout the Borough, in addition to the Anderson shelters designed for individual households. These were to be freely used throughout the air raids, with the one under the Odeon Cinema being in constant use. As lorries began to convey sand from the local quarries to London, both hospitals were amongst the first buildings to be sandbagged in the town.

From the first day of war, the railway station was called upon to meet very heavy demands. Initially it was the many thousands of troops heading to the Continent, as members of the Expeditionary Force. And this large-scale movement involved thousands of tons of equipment, which was most efficiently handled and processed through the goods yard. Later again in 1940 the station handled massive movements of troops, but this time in a more sombre mood as the evacuation from Dunkirk gathered momentum. Throughout the war until after the cessation of hostilities, troops either in special trains or travelling in small parties or singly, of every nation in the Allied cause, passed through Redhill. It was to become a common sight, soldiers in a variety of international uniforms and talking strange languages and dialects. Though the station was never seriously threatened from the air, there were occasional attempts by stray planes, but the bombs fell elsewhere.

The Borough was generally considered to be a 'safe area' in terms of the possibility of air raids, though it was accepted that the town would receive some attention from the skies. It was therefore felt there was no need to evacuate children, but every precaution was made to protect schools and provide air raid shelters. As a 'safe area', the Borough was automatically a reception centre and the first evacuee children arrived from London on 3rd September 1939. It was the beginning of a massive evacuation that within months was to reach a peak of 5000. Apart from the children billeted on householders, the Council opened nine hostels and made arrangements for parents to visit them at weekends. When the expected air raids in London did not materialise, there was a general return to the city. By February the following year the number of evacuee children had been reduced to under 3000.

From the start it was decided to form a Home Guard and the response was magnificent. In the Borough over 800 joined and the local unit eventually reached battalion strength. They were used in various capacities, including the need to watch out for parachutists, who might be dropped to carry out sabotage work at nights. Some of the volunteers were not accustomed to rifles and tended to swing them around, when practising loading and unloading. At least one guardroom floor was punctured when a young volunteer, after unloading at the end of the night, pulled the trigger to make sure that "he hadn't left one in"! This incident may or may not have been responsible for an order that was later issued. Effectively, the five rounds issued to each man had to be carried in the pocket and only loaded into the weapon when, "the Volunteer is confronted by the enemy"!

After the outbreak of war, it was also expected that air raids would swiftly follow. When they did not, it was almost an anti-climax. In fact, Britain had entered a period that was later called 'the phoney war'.

Throughout the winter of 1939/40, there were no German air raids to disturb the tranquility of the British Isles. It was as if there was no war at all. There were, however, good reasons for this status quo. For at the time the German air force, the Luftwaffe, was cast in the role of a support force for the army. This combination of fire-power proved extremely effective in Poland and was later used in Norway, the Low countries and France with similar success. In fact Germany did not consider that air attacks launched from home bases would have any effect on British targets. As the Royal Air Force was still relatively weak, Britain saw no point inviting retaliation by carrying out raids on the German fatherland.

Christmas that year seemed as it had always been, but gradually one by one, social facilities were being withdrawn as civilian labour became scarce. Life in Redhill as people had known it in peacetime was no more. But like everyone else in the country, the community adapted to the new way of life without too much hardship. There were changes to get used to and unusual visitors to accept. Such as Billingsgate Fish Market, that arrived and took over the old brewery buildings at Linkfield Corner for a couple of weeks, before returning to London.

In February PC "Jock" Mason was seconded for ARP duties, with specific responsibilities to purchase and modify secondhand vehicles for use as ambulances. He was also responsible for testing and assessing the driving skills of the volunteers.

"I was instructed to test and assess several dozen car owners, who had volunteered to drive Civil Defence ambulances in the event of war. The list of names comprised women from all classes of society, including the Mayoress of Reigate, magistrates, town councillors, housewives, shop and office girls. ....I decided to use a 30cwt Ford van for the purpose of testing. The first tests proved that many of the drivers were quite unsuited to that type of vehicle. Some had such short legs that they had to pack cushions behind their backs, in order to allow their feet to reach the control pedals".

Several weeks of practice and training produced many competent drivers of both sexes, but there were problems. When a few of the women were told that their standard of driving was not up to "scratch", they "flew into a temper with frustration". Mason felt he should approach the Medical Officer of Health, Dr Bingham, for advice but the reply was uncompromising;

"There is probably a clinical reason for such behaviour, but under the present circumstances it is a problem you will have to solve yourself".

Despite the teething problems, the unit was soon efficiently organised and a number of cars purchased. These were sent to John Chalmers & Sons in the High Street for conversion to ambulances, at "a cost not exceeding £30 per vehicle". One of the ambulance depots was at the Sewage Disposal Works in Earlswood, where conditions left much to be desired.

"The intolerable conditions prevailing at the depot were even worse than the Reigate depot, due to vermin and unsanitary personal accommodation. Eventually permission was granted to transfer the depot to the sports ground in the town".

The winter passed giving way to spring; a spring in which the iron fist of the Wehrmacht smashed the armies of Holland, Belgium and France, laying waste their countries. Even then no German raiders crossed English skies. For it was not until the German army had finally crushed the French and delivered the British army a devastating blow at Dunkirk, did the Luftwaffe turn its attention to England. But even then, the opportunities for bombing the troop trains evacuating the army from Dunkirk were not taken.

Whitsun seemed normal enough with the trains and buses full of holiday-makers. But news from the front was not good. The war was not going well and it was becoming increasingly obvious that there would have to be a massive evacuation of the British Army from France. On 26th May the Southern Railway Company received the code word "Dynamo", the signal the evacuation had started. Two days later the churches in the Borough were packed as a Day of National Prayer was held; there was now a very real danger of invasion. And this was made more apparent when road signposts and town nameplates were removed.

In Redhill the station was closed to all normal traffic for the first time in its history, as preparations were made to receive troops from the Kent coast. For local people some trains operated to Merstham, while Earlswood station remained open to cater for passengers from London and Brighton on the loop line. During the next ten days the movement of troops, mostly without equipment, continued day and night through the station. Redhill was effectively the focal point and during this hectic period handled over 600 trains and 300,000 troops. Almost all the engines had to be coaled and watered before continuing to various destinations. Speed was essential and the trains were often cleared in four minutes. During the brief stopover, the local WVS and members of the Rotary clubs of Redhill and Reigate were on hand to provide refreshments. Tens of thousands of cups of tea, sandwiches and cakes were provided for the weary soldiers. Never had England seen such scenes as were witnessed at Redhill that May. As each train drew up to the platform, greatcoats and tunics were hanging from the windows of the carriage doors to dry; still wet from the sea at Dunkirk as soldiers had waded to the boats. In the carriages the men tired, dishevelled and some bandaged, still managed smiles and words of thanks as they gulped down cups of tea. It was as one young WVS helper remarked later, "an experience I never want to go through again". During the war the WVS operated two regular canteens in the Borough, including one at Marketfield which was opened for all service personnel and later moved to St. Matthew's Mission Hall. Apart from the tremendous work for all the evacuating troops from Dunkirk, they provided hospitality for over two million members of the forces.

In June the London defences were pierced and soon afterwards Kenley was attacked. Aerial 'dog fights' erupted over Redhill, Reigate and Merstham. The Battle of Britain had begun.

On August 15th the Borough received its baptism of fire in the first of a series of mass raids. Within an hour no fewer than 125 bombs were dropped but, fortunately, with no more serious injury than three cyclists, who were blown from their machines by the blast of an explosion. The sirens sounded again in the evening and over thirty enemy aircraft were engaged by Spitfires. Again dog fights erupted all over the Borough and onlookers were at last rewarded when three enemy aircraft, including a Dornier, were shot down. But exciting though the spectacle of a dog fight might have been watched safely from the ground, the reality of death was another matter. So far Redhill had escaped but not for much longer. Soon after lunch on August 18th the sirens sounded and the explosions swiftly followed. Fourteen bombs were dropped in a line between Church Street in Reigate and Hatchlands Road. One of them fell in the centre of the roadway at Shaw's Corner and five people were killed. The windows of nearby houses were shattered and the Foresters Arms slightly damaged. It was just the beginning, for many more were to die or be maimed and injured. Keeping an eye on the skies became routine, for death was never far away.

Throughout September the air raids intensified, with bombs falling in many areas of the Borough. A stick of bombs came down in the Wiggey area and the Frenches Road School had all its windows blown out. A few days later an attack on Earlswood station was unsuccessful, but a bomb scored a direct hit on the main outfall sewer on the Common and made a 60-foot crater. Touring damage caused by one air raid, the Mayor, H.J. Hamblen, remarked;

"It was most amazing the calm displayed
by young and old alike. It is something
this country can be really proud of".

On the 23rd two bombs came down near the Nags Head, fracturing the water mains and blocking the Brighton Road. If September had been bad,

October was worse and as many as eight warnings a day were common. Most of the raids were indiscriminate and the Surrey Mirror was quick to headline them, as well as the intensity of the bombings; "LONE RAIDERS"; "INDISCRIMINATE RAIDS"; "A NIGHT OF INTENSE ACTIVITY" and "HAPHAZARD BOMBING", were headlines that reflected the traumas of life in Redhill that October.

While large scale air raids could be detected, the occasional lone raider getting through without much warning was always a danger. On 6th October one made a deliberate attack on Redhill station, but the bombs came down in the goods yard at Hooley and Brook Road. The raider then sped off, dropping four in Garlands Road and one on a house in Ridgeway Road, which passed through the roof and out into the front garden without exploding. Having got rid of his load, the raider turned northwards and just for good measure, put a cannon shell through the roof of the Odeon Cinema.

By now no area was safe and during the ensuing weeks, delayed action and incendiary bombs fell near the East Surrey Hospital and in Meadvale. The Earlswood area came in for particular attention and direct hits were made on properties in Earlsbrook and Victoria roads. But the worst raid was on the 27th, when a 1000lb bomb completely destroyed five houses in Emlyn Road and severely damaged 110 others. Six people were killed and over twentyfour injured.

By November Jock Mason and his ambulance unit were working flatout with little respite. The daily log book was now recording an increasing number of incidents, though not all of a war nature. For despite valiant efforts to get rid of the vermin, the problem still remained.

"Tuesday 12th.....The mice have now returned to this depot".
And three days later...."further complaints from the night staff of the mice".

Throughout 1941 air raid warnings gradually diminished and by May, night-time raids had practically ceased. This was mainly due to the new night fighters, which scored spectacular success against the enemy. Based at Redhill Aerodrome, 219 Squadron were in constant action attacking aircraft using the line to London, from Beachy Head in Sussex. But there continued to be heavy daytime raids and the toll of civilian casualties remorselessly mounted.

By May the ambulance service had reached a strength of eighty personnel and a total of twenty vehicles capable of carrying casualties. April had been one of the busiest months, with 61 incidents and over 440 bombs dropped. This had placed the service under extreme pressure, but the ambulance teams with Jock Mason, in charge, were able to meet the challenge.

Problems continued to arise with pilfering of petrol and the non-return of blankets, as well as stretchers which were in short supply. Somehow the ambulances kept going, despite damaged self-starters and the continual search for spare parts.

In May with the arrival in the skies of the new night-fighters, it was a relief when air raid warnings decreased and finally ceased for a time. Though morale and alertness remained high generally, a few in the ambulance service thought it time to relax, in particular the elderly lady member who told Jock that she deserved a holiday.

> "She stated that if I did not arrange to cover her duties, she would send in her resignation. I said, 'don't worry sending it in, I will accept it now!' When she brought in her equipment, I said, 'thank you madam. All we want now is a bomb at your front door'.
> A few months later a bomb did drop a few hundred yards from her house, but she was not badly injured. When the ambulance arrived she said to the driver, 'tell PC Mason I've had it. He will understand!'"

But not all casualties were results of air raids. In Merstham an old age pensioner died after forgetting to light his gas fire. At the inquest the coroner remarked that it was tragic to die in this way, particularly as the old man had, "never needed a doctor in the whole of his 92 years". In answer to a question, the son replied that his father had often said to him, "a glass of beer a day will keep you alive a long time".

And helping to keep Redhill's citizens alive that year were a fresh batch of troops, mainly Canadian. Stationed in various parts of the Borough, their presence was to assist with defence by manning anti-aircraft guns and other strong points in case of attack. They also helped in local events and raised money for the Spitfire Fund by playing baseball at the Memorial Sports Ground. One of their most auspicious occasions was when King George made a visit to the town and presented them with colours. It was an honour they richly deserved and warmly welcomed by the people of Redhill, with whom they made many life-long friends. In September, as rationing began to bite even harder, those of the community who still ran cars for private use found that half a gallon was all they could get for the following month. But this did not effect firms who were involved with the war effort; firms like Redhill Tile Company, who produced over 300,000 4.2inch mortar bombs and 4.5 inch shells.

By 1942 Redhill had become so accustomed to incidents, that it came as a pleasant respite when the year turned out to be "bomb free". Though warnings continued, there was only one incident when a Focke-Wulf strafed a train and a bus, but this caused little damage and no casualties. And this respite enabled Jock Mason to concentrate on the routine duties of the unit, which included maintaining a reasonable standard of cleanliness at the depot. In May he was far from happy with the situation.

"The Ambulance Officer is very much concerned with regard to the filthy condition of a pillow slip. This was quite recently put into the dormitory to be used as a pillow and not as a doormat".

However, he made a point of congratulating a couple of members of the unit for their efforts. But another member who was not mentioned, took exception and made an entry in the report book.

"A PROTEST - I wish to state in writing that I strongly object to the Ambulance Officer's uncalled for remarks re cleanliness. The floor of the Parade Room only became filthy after two months of neglect, due to shortage of polish and floor cloths. In repeated requests for some by personnel, they were informed that the floor polish had been 'mislaid' in the Ambulance Officer's car".

Obviously this could not be left unanswered.

"There appears to be some misunderstanding among certain members of the personnel, regarding whose responsibility it is to clean the depot. Instructions were issued and duties until recently performed well. Now there has been a 'slackening off', with the result that the standard of

> cleanliness required by the Ambulance Officer, has been permitted to fall to a very low level. He was therefore within his authority, to draw attention to the 'filthy' condition of the depot. Accordingly, he will continue to maintain discipline and stamp out insubordination".

Though the general standard of cleanliness improved, there still existed an "unpleasant odour". An inspection by the Borough Surveyor's department ruled out that it was due to "Dead Rats etc". However, a few days later the mystery was solved.

> "This has at last been traced to the cheap lamp shade in the office, which is chiefly comprised of fish glue".

In 1943 the iron railings surrounding properties were taken away to meet national needs. Another sacrifice was when The Ring on Earlswood Common and parts of the other Commons, were ploughed up to grow crops. But there were signs that the war was changing for the better, when Italian prisoners of war were seen being marched through the streets and put to work at the Refuse Disposal Works. And other signs too, when only a handful of air raids occurred during the year.

Sadly it was but another respite. For during the early months of 1944 there were over fifty alerts, though only the occasional bomb was dropped. However, a more sinister danger was to appear; the flying bomb.

The first one came down harmlessly enough on a tree at the Philanthropic School. But two nights later the second had fatal effects, when it demolished a house on the corner of Earlsbrook Road and St, John's Road and damaged several others. There had been little warning and with residents asleep in their beds, over ten lost their lives. Serious though the haphazard bombing had been, the flying bombs presented a much greater threat. In July the voluntary evacuation of children from the Borough was ordered and over 5000 left, for destinations in the West Country and Wales. And amongst them was young Bob Colins from Grove Road.

Towards the end of August the flying bomb menace finally came to an end, leaving a total of 23 killed and sixty five injured. In the two months period, seventeen bombs came down in the Borough and such was the intensity of their explosions, that 40 houses were completely destroyed, 120 seriously damaged and 1400 slightly damaged. By the end of November with no more incidents of any kind, most of the children were able to return in time for Christmas. And returning, too, were many Redhill men who had fought in North Africa and elsewhere, only to be captured and made prisoners of war. Some had escaped and made their way to Switzerland and it was these men, who now found themselves unexpectedly feted by the town. And being officially welcomed by no less a person than the Mayor himself, Alderman A. Windsor-Spice, who presented them with gifts. It was the town's mark of appreciation to its loyal sons, who had answered the call of duty and safely returned. For those who did not, the Cenotaph at Shaw's Corner once again recorded with honour their names for posterity.

With Christmas approaching advertisements abounded. Logs for the fire could be bought from Charles Lock of Hooley Lane for 35/- a load, delivered. In Blackborough Road a lady was generously offering a live-in maid,"£2 weekly plus insurance, in a comfortable home". And for the wealthy, comfortable homes were being offered for sale.

"Attractive residence, Earlswood Common,
consisting 6-7 beds, 2 baths, 3 Rec etc,
garages, stabling and cottage, 1ë acres
£5,500".

Down town, despite the limitations that war had brought, the people of Redhill were preparing for Christmas. After all, with daily good news from the battlefronts, it looked as if the war might be over before long. Perhaps it was still too early to celebrate, but the rich lady in Blackborough Road could afford to buy her husband a bottle of Johnny Walker Black Label whisky for 27/9d.

As hostilities came to an end, a report on incidents which occurred in the Borough during the war was issued.

Civilian casualties: 50 killed, 161 injured.
Houses destroyed: 115, damaged 4189.
Alerts: 893.
High explosive bombs 496; oil bombs 18; incendiary bombs 5847; flying bombs 17.

It was a fearful cost, but only a fraction of what the whole of England had suffered. Now, at last, eyes need no longer be cast at the skies, nor the sirens wail out. No more the sounds of droning planes and crashing bombs; gone too the fearful swishing of the flying bomb and the devastation of death; silent at last the tolling bells, as Redhill laid her dead to rest. For now the dark chapter of war was closed and ahead the prospect of peace and a new beginning.

Throughout the Borough, children's street parties were organised to celebrate the end of hostilities. Once again Windsor-Spice made a point of attending them, even after days of official functions. He was, as one old resident put it, "a quite remarkable man. Boundless energy and always keen to be with the people".

On the Sunday following VE Day, a parade of military, civil defence, ex-service and youth organisations was held at the Memorial Sports Ground. Over 3000 men, women and youngsters attended, while churches everywhere were filled with people giving thanks. There was as there had been almost thirty years previously, "a sense of hope for the future; a new beginning".

The Railway Underground Nerve Centre in 1940. (courtesy Jack Reeves)

REDHILL FROM THE AIR. (A 818).

Photograph   EARLSWOOD INCIDENT BY FLYING BOMB   *A. Windsor-Spice Ltd.*
June 19th, 1944
(courtesy Jack Sales)

In 1948 the Brighton Road was widened at its junction with Hooley Lane, when the old wooden fence was replaced with a brick wall to surround the Sea Cadet's Headquarters. The property was originally "Shenley", an imposing house owned by the Foster family. In 1938 the house was used to accommodate Jewish refugees from Europe.
(courtesy Redhill Library)

The Town Centre in 1967
(courtesy Redhill Library)

Chapter 10
A TOWN OF CHANGE

The Second Word War labelled in some circle as "the war to end all wars", was proved completely wrong only a few short years later, with the outbreak of the Korean War. It was a parochial war insofar as it remained within the boundaries of Korea; but in reality it was another world war that fortunately for mankind, did not expand beyond those boundaries. It was bloody and fierce, taking a terrible toll of young lives again, but ending almost as abruptly as it had started. In a way it brought people to their senses and from it grew and developed the Cold War. In another sense the Korean War did not seriously effect the post-war recovery process in England, where the welfare state had made a tentative start. It was a concept that in 1919 had been considered Utopian in outlook. For though the Great War had shaken the social framework to its foundations, old fashioned Victorian individualism remained. The Depression and World War II changed all that, because the children of the twenties who had fought in the second conflict demanded security from poverty. Now with a Labour Government and radically changed attitudes, it became a reality.

It could be said that a person who had gone to sleep in 1950 and then woken up in 1990, would not have seen many changes. Cars, planes, radios and televisions would have dramatically improved, but there would have been no quantum leap. Even space travel would not have appeared exceptional to anyone who had witnessed the German V2 rockets over England and their post-war development. But what would not have been recognisable, would have been films, books, magazines, videos and their explicit sex; the universal acceptance of divorce, "living in sin" and single parenthood.

And for the Redhill person who had gone to sleep in 1950 and woken up in 1990, the town would have been unrecognisable. For though the process of re-development took some years to evolve, the end result was a completely re-designed town centre.

But in 1946 it was back to routine police work for Jock Mason and soon there was an incident to deal with on Earlswood Common. A pony had strayed on to the road and was unfortunately knocked down by a car. There was little the vet could do and he decided the pony should be destroyed to save it further suffering. As he was making the arrangements with Mason, a somewhat drunken horse dealer arrived and became very abusive. In fact he informed the vet that if the pony was shot, he would deliver him 'a punch on the nose.' At that, Mason took the man by the shoulder and told him, "if anyone is to be punched on the nose, punch me on the nose here and now". And that settled the matter. Animals wandering on to main roads continued to be a problem, as was the case when a cow decided to lie down in the middle of the Brighton Road and go to sleep. This turned out to be the cow's last sleep, for a bus driver on his way from Horley to Redhill, missed seeing the poor animal in the dark and ran over it.

The late forties were years of planning not just for the postwar population explosion, but the influx of hundreds of "bombed out" families from London who needed to be re-housed. It was a period when the Big Freeze hit the Borough so badly, that communications were disrupted on a massive scale as the temperature plunged to an incredible -17 Celsius. A period as businesses gradually "got back on their feet" or moved to new locations, like the Surrey Value Company did in 1948, when they acquired bigger premises in Brighton Road. But it was also a re-adjustment period for families, disrupted by the war and in many cases separated from loved ones. Some never did re-adjust, but for Arthur King and his wife Mary the immediate post-war years gave them wonderful opportunities to share things together. And going to the cinema was one of these experiences, even with a toothache.

The tooth had been hurting for a week, but Arthur had avoided visiting the dentist. He kept making excuses hoping the tooth would somehow mend itself. The pain eased a little as he walked towards Redhill General, but then came on strong as he arrived.

"I went to meet the wife one Saturday night over at the hospital. She says, 'we'll go to the pictures tonight'. George Formby in KEEP YOUR SEATS PLEASE was on. Oh! my tooth - well it was real rotten; right down to the gum, a double one. And I was miserable.
She says, 'you're having the tooth out Monday'.
I said, 'oh! yes', brave as you like, knowing the dentist was closed Mondays.
We went down the Brighton Road. All of a sudden she dived into a

doorway and pressed the bell.
I said, 'what are you doing?'
She says, 'there's a dentist up here. You're having your tooth out'.
I said, 'no, its alright'. But it was aching like hell.
Anyway, he came down and said, 'I'm sorry but I can't do it right now. Can you come back in half an hour?'
I said, 'oh! yes'.
The wife hadn't heard this and I came out and said, 'no he can't do it, he's booked up'.
'oh! alright', she said.
Well, we got to the Pavilion and I said, 'come on we'll go in'.
She says, 'no. I want to look in Jones'.
Little did I know there was a dentist right next door. She went in there and pressed the bell. I said, 'what are you doing?'
'There's a dentist in there'.
He came out. 'Oh! yes come in', he said. 'I'll take you straight away'.
Well, he took it out. Oh! it was a relief when it was out. And my face was out here. And of course George Formby was on and me laughing and me face jumping up and down. That was the first tooth I'd had out and I was real scared.
He said, 'I wish all my patients sat as still as you'.
I said, 'they're probably not as scared as I was!'"

With the completion in South Merstham of some 1500 houses designed to accommodate six thousand people, the population almost doubled. This sizeable 'invasion' created problems and in particular with the older residents, who had lived in the village for generations. For a time there was friction and a certain amount of tension, which inevitably led to a "them and us" situation. But the development in South Merstham had been well planned and gradually the new arrivals were absorbed into the community. In time the skills and way of life they brought with them were to enrich the neighbourhood, a contribution which is very evident today.

But not everything was going smoothly, least of all the nationalised electricity services. Following a serious electricity failure in April 1950, an angry Surrey Mirror reader wrote

"Sir,- If ever anybody wanted evidence of the disadvantages

of Nationalisation they certainly had it on Wednesday morning, if they lived in Reigate Borough. An early telephone call to the South Eastern Electricity Board could elicit no information as to when the supply would be restored.

....When electricity was generated locally, the inhabitants of the Borough never suffered such an utter and complete breakdown".

However, electricity failures were far from young Bob Collins' thoughts as he grew up in Grove Road, where he had been born in 1940. Like Mrs Gardiner many years before, he clearly remembers the rows of grim terraced houses.

"There was a doss house across the road. It was a rough old road of terraced houses, just like Coronation Street with everyone looking out the windows".

As a young boy he went to school in Cromwell Road and earned a few pennies on Saturdays, by making deliveries for Coopers the greengrocers. In particular he remembers at the end of a hard day, regularly making his last delivery of a sack of potatoes to Miss Star at the Home Cottage.

"I had to lug his heavy sack up flights of steps for 6d and a bar of chocolate. That's what she gave me every Saturday night. About six o'clock it was and I'd been working since eight in the morning. The Brighton Road was busy then but safer than today. All small shops and houses. Quintons and Chandlers the wet fish shop. Then there was St. Matthew's Parish Rooms, where I used to be in the Church Lads Brigade. I wanted to be a drummer but then I got stuck being a bugler. Used to ride our old soap boxes on wheels from the top of Sincots Road, do a right into Grove Road down to the bottom and then come to a stop at the Royal Oak. The only money we ever got was a penny or twopence collection money for church. Every Sunday we had to go without fail. We were bloody poor then but my father and mother looked after us alright. He never went out much, except for a couple of drinks on a Saturday night. They both smoked Woodbines or Weights, packets of five they were. And my mother caught me smoking once and didn't half hit me over the head with an enamel pan.

The other memory I have is of old Jack Harber the rag and bone man. He used to live on the corner of Grove Road. Kept a horse and cart there and there was a stables at the back. Then my grandfather lived in the next house. I don't know what he did, but he seemed to survive. He used to take us out rabbitting over the fields where Warwick School is now and beyond there. Seven Fields we called it. Then there was the brook, Gurney's Brook, though some call it different. We used to polevault over it and float tin baths in it. I always remember that brook, because my mum lost her temper one day and threw my roller skates in it. You used to be able to get to the brook by walking down Chandler's Alley, the old path opposite Grove Road. But that's gone now, after they built the parade of shops. It was a right of way and you got all the way to Lakers, by going through the tunnel under the railway''.

With business now back on a more normal footing, John Stoneman & Sons purchased Doran Court near Shaw's Corner and converted the old house into a funeral home. And this was a welcome change from the demolition that was taking place elsewhere, particularly as parts of the house dated back to 1731. At that time it had been owned by Thomas Burt and known as Ganders, but in 1748 it was renamed The Hatch and this name continued until 1907.

Also in the news was Alan Bristow, when he launched his new company Bristow Helicopters and established his administrative headquarters at Redhill Aerodrome. But the major event of 1951 was the Festival of Britain. A number of functions were staged in the Borough and the money raised, was given to the Mayor's Appeal for the building of additional almshouses in Redhill. And it is this spirit of "giving" which has always been such an important part of the Redhill character; as it was clearly shown during the Coronation celebrations, which included scores of street parties and charitable events.

This could also be said of Grices the bakers, when they celebrated their Diamond Jubilee in 1954. For nearly 3500 currant spiced buns were distributed to all the elementary schools, "to be eaten with the children's mid-morning milk". One of the most notable members of the family was William Grice, who in his younger years, had been a founder member of the Redhill Bowling Club.

And it was at the game that he gained international fame, when he skipped an unbeaten England team in 1932 and 1933. Further fame followed in 1939, when he won the Coronation Cup as single-handed champion of Great Britain in, "the largest single-handed bowls contest in the world". But in 1954 it was Vic Stone of Earlswood who was the sports hero, when he was awarded the Polytechnic's Studd Trophy as Sportsman of the Year. As an international walker for England, he had just completed twenty years in competitive events. He was a man of considerable stamina and a member of the exclusive Centurians, which set a standard of walking 100 miles in 24 hours under competitive rules.

And there was more good news in 1955 when, following a 6-1 trouncing of Hitchin the previous week, Redhill Football Club completed a successful Easter weekend programme, by defeating Sutton United 2-1 on the Saturday and Barnet 1-0 on the Monday. But the Reigate-Redhill News warned that the "Reds" were apt to show complacency and that their 2-0 loss to Cambridge earlier in the season, should be taken seriously. However, they did manage to reach the 3rd round of the FA Amateur Cup and drew a crowd of nearly 6000 at the Memorial Ground for their encounter with Hendon. But any thoughts of Wembley were quickly shattered when the visitors won comfortably by six goals to nil. Not that football was on people's minds when they queued up for the 2nd Reigate Troop's jumble sale at the Scout Hut, Earlswood. For here were bargains galore and this held true soon after the doors opened, when a fifty year old gramophone horn sold for 3d. And there were other great bargains too, including a violin for £1 and a chest of drawers which fetched ten shillings. But April was also a month for jobs, with Redhill General Hospital encouraging the fairer sex to take up a nursing career. However, those applying might have interpreted the wording of the advertisement to imply that they were needed to care for injured actors.

"Young ladies 18-30 are offered every facility
to train as Student Nurses for the examination
to enter the Stage Register. The course lasts
3 years. Salary during this time £225-£250 pa,
less £103 for board/lodging".

Presumably any young lady jumping at this opportunity, would soon be sampling the culinary delights of the hospital's new cook, who had just been employed on a basic wage of £8 per week.

In May the Council announced that their plans were well advanced for providing more local light industry and, as a consequence, more jobs. Six new factories were to be built at Holmethorpe and areas of the Brighton Road had also been earmarked for development. At a meeting the Mayor said that, "more industry in the Borough would reduce the number of people who were at present forced to travel to find work. Many share my view, that people should have local employment and not use the trains". This was not a view shared by the Board of Trade in London who objected that, "there is not sufficient population locally to support more industry".

In turn, this opinion was certainly not shared by Foxboro-Yoxhall Instruments, who purchased 58 acres of land at Wiggey. By 1958 the complex was fully established and the company employing around 1000 staff. And Woolworths had every confidence in the future, when they announced in June that they intended to double the size of their store in the High Street. In order for this to happen, the old houses in Rees Road would be demolished and the road itself disappear from the town map. Already an area at the back of Rees Road had been cleared for future development and it would not be too many years, before a section of Ladbroke Road received a similar fate. But for the time being G.H. Carver could carry on his business there. And this was welcomed by the gambling fraternity who did not want to be seen coming out of bookmakers premises; particularly by the wife. This problem was recognised by Mr Carver who decided to offer customers, "Business by Telephone and Post only". No problem there; in fact he assured clients that they could, "Bet with Security and Civility" and urged that they,

"Don't delay, Bet today, Just lift
the Receiver and I will Pay".

But in the Borough libraries it was the bookworms who held the limelight, when the Librarian reported that there had been a considerable increase in borrowers and "the issue of books in Redhill was larger than that of Reigate, though tastes were very different".

And tastes were certainly different at the Greyhound pub in Brighton Road on Wednesday nights, where the landlord held swinging sessions for the younger generation. With the Embers Jazz Band in attendance, it was the "in place" to be and as one young lady remarked, "filled a blank in the entertainment provided in the Redhill area". Not that cinemagoers would have agreed, for after the Pavilion in the High Street closed down, the Odeon became the sole cinema in town providing, "nothing but the best". Capable of seating nearly 1500 patrons, it was the main venue for popular entertainment, particularly amongst the youngsters. Commenting on the massive cleaning operation that was needed to keep the cinema "spic and span", a member of the staff added;

> "not only is litter left by the customers; we have found some of the most extraordinary articles. Once a wooden leg was left behind and was never claimed by its owner. Also unclaimed was a set of false teeth. Perhaps the owner was too embarrassed to call for them".

Apart from some noisy behaviour, cinema shows were usually incident-free as were bus journeys, though occasionally conductors had to keep an eye on "rowdy bands of school children". But it was not school children who caused problems on the 405 one January morning; it was a sack of coal and an old man called Eustace. Hardly headline news, but the story did touch the hearts of many when they read about it in the Reigate-Redhill News.

> "Eustace boarded a 405 bus outside Redhill and put his sack of coal on to the platform. He then decided to go upstairs for the journey. But the conductor called him back. For, as everyone should know, a bag of coal on the platform of a bus is sure to get in the way of passengers. But apparently Eustace did not see it that way and refused to move his fuel.
> And for his obstinancy, he appeared at the Borough Court charged with 'placing a bulky article elsewhere than directed by the conductor'. And Eustace was fined £2 by the magistrates. So evidence was formally given.
> The conductor, who was so stern with Eustace, told the court that the defendant boarded the bus at the stop past Redhill Market Place. Eustace was said to have flung his sack of coal on to the platform and to have started to go upstairs.
> 'I told him to take it upstairs with him', the conductor claimed. Whereupon Eustace made a rude reply - telling the conductor to go somewhere most unpleasant.
> So the conductor became stern and told the defendant that

he would call a policeman, if he did not move he coal off the platform within five minutes. But according to the conductor, Eustace replied;

'You can call the police now, I am not going to move the sack'. When the policeman arrived, the conductor informed him that he was not prepared to take Eustace any further. So about 20 minutes after the trouble had first started, the bus continued on its way - the conductor having removed Eustace's coal himself. One of the passengers said that Eustace couldn't have put his sack in the luggage compartment, as a woman had already placed a large suitcase there. The passenger said he heard the conductor tell Eustace to take the sack upstairs, to which the response was; 'I'm not prepared to remove the coal for you or anyone else'.

Detective McKenzie told the court that Eustace admitted to the offence. However, if the conductor had removed his ticket box from the luggage rack, there would have been room for the sack".

And so, sadly, Eustace left the dock to return to the warmth of his coal fire. He certainly would make a point of avoiding the stern conductor and the 405 in the future. While on the bench the magistrates nodded in agreement, that they had dealt with another "serious case" satisfactorily. But the bus conductor on the 405 was not the only one having problems. For when his mate on the 439 to Reigate told a small girl to stop ringing the bell, the child's mother became quite abusive.

"How dare you! You uncouth, lowdown, country busman you!" After being fined in court for using "offensive language", the woman was asked why she had spoken to the conductor in such a manner.

"Because he looked in a fearful rage. Besides, I don't think the conductor has a very happy countenance".

Cruel words! After all, he was hardly responsible for the way he looked. At least Their Honours on the bench had fewer problems with the next lady to appear before them for exceeding the speed limit. Most of the speeding offences which came before the court were dealt with quickly, as defendants admitted they had not realised they had been travelling so fast. The case of the good lady from Leigh was also processed with speed, but her explanation was somewhat different.

> "It is the first time in a blameless life", she told the policeman when he stopped her in Doversgreen Road.
> "I was following that one", she added, pointing to a passing helicopter.

It was certainly a busy month for the courts, though most of the cases were of a relatively minor nature. One man who had been summoned for parking between a zebra crossing and a road sign, sent a letter stating that he had enclosed a postal order for ten shillings and hoping, "this meets with your approval".
Obviously it did not, for he was fined £1.

Two days later Showbiz came to court, in the form of Sam Costa the well-known stage and radio personality. Finding himself another victim of Redhill's notorious speed trap, he told the officer who stopped him that he "honestly never saw the signs. That means I will get one - that's the first time". But Sam got two instead. He was fined £2.

But for Bob Collins speeding was never a problem in the late fifties, for like other young men he just could not afford a car. It was very much a case of having to walk or take a bus. But this presented no problems since he worked on the railways and it was only a short walk to his favourite haunt, the Britannia Inn in Brighton Road.

> "It was a real pub, no optics in those days, just beer and a big open fire. And me and my mates would go there of a Saturday night and didn't go home until Sunday. Wally the landlord would say, 'well I'm going to lock up and go to bed. There's a couple of crates out the back'. And he'd go to bed and we'd sit there all night and settle up with him in the morning. It was a great pub. Used to organise coach trips and many a time I went on them. They were always Graves the garage people's coaches and were all white".

Sadly the Britannia has passed into history and so too has the Royal Oak, which for so long had been part of the High Street scene. In November 1957 it finally closed its doors and its licence was transferred to the newly-opened Monson Arms. Sad though the occasion was, the landlord arranged a lively skiffle group whose final rendition of the National Anthem, was sung with feeling by all present. As an old regular recalled;

> "This was done as a last salute to a happy crowd and the end of an era at the Royal Oak. When the last orders were called, it really meant last orders".

In December 1958 plans were afoot to ease the traffic problem in the town centre and create a pedestrian mall. At this stage it was all talk, but the concept of constructing a by-pass was very much on people's minds. The following year the overall plans were approved by the County Council for the re-development of the town centre, subject to "detailed investigations". For businessmen it was a matter of "wait and see" and getting on with their jobs, or, in the case of Lambert and Sons, changing ownership of the High Street bakers and confectioners. And with the retirement of Eric Lambert, there ended the family association with the area, that had begun so long ago at the Blackborough Mill. For H & A Trower the Earlswood seed merchants, 1959 was a bad year, when fire ripped through their warehouse completely destroying the old building. A new steel and concrete structure was erected and the company continued trading for some years. In 1993 the site was re-developed and several blocks of flats built.

Throughout the sixties the development of the town centre continued to be a contentious issue, as proposals were put forward and either amended or delayed for one reason or another. Admittedly it was important to produce a plan that was best for Redhill, but there were a number of issues involved and many people who would be affected. This in particular applied to the by-pass proposals, where any suggestion to cut through the Memorial Sports Ground was vehemently opposed. And with good reason, for the ground had been a gift to the people of the town. There was also opposition to the proposed demolition of the Colman Institute, obliteration of Cecil Road and the removal of a sizable section of Ladbroke Road. In addition, the interests of the people who lived or had businesses there had to be taken into consideration. And among them was Redhill Football Club, already supported by 15,000 signatures, whose facilities would be decimated.

Some plans had already been approved, including the Cromwell Road Estate development and the central car park. At the helm had been the retiring

Chief Engineer and Surveyor George Sanderson, under whose guidance the estates at The Dome and Colesmead had been built. In the private sector there was less of a problem.

> "In Station Road and the High Street, the old is disappearing and yielding to the new. The vast unloveliness of the gas works has vanished, although the capacious gasholders of Hooley Lane remain. And an area of many acres is being made ripe for development. Private developers have been active on the slope of Redstone Hill, in the area between Linkfield Lane and Gatton Park Road and latterly on both sides of Batts Hill, as well as conducting 'infilling' in many old spaces in all parts of the Borough".

Meanwhile the public were more interested in other matters, such as Kennards "Special Offer" of fireside chairs

> "A really comfortable chair with latex back, loose latex seat on tension spring. Covered uncut Moquette in assorted colourings. Normally £6.15.0. AT SPECIAL PRICE £5.19.6."

But for the musically-minded, Semprini's Recital at the Market Hall was "sheer bliss from a master artist". And apart from being a complete sell out, it raised a considerable amount of money in aid of the Redhill and Reigate Nursing Division of the St. John's Ambulance Brigade. The concert was one of several he gave for charity, as well as marking his close association as a resident of Millway.

However, concerts and shop sales were far from people's thoughts in January 1963, when they woke on New Year's Day to find a thick blanket of snow. But this was not surprising as snow had been falling since just after Christmas, in what was described as the worst blizzard since 1947. There was also a severe frost, which caused 1000 consumers in the area of the East Surrey Water Company to be without supplies for several days. Plumbers were called out on numerous occasions and by the time conditions improved, they had dealt with 250 burst pipes. In fact the weather was so cold that the Surrey Mirror printed a souvenir card on the frozen Earlswood lakes, to commemorate the unknown printer who on the same day in 1739, plied his trade on the Thames ice. And there was more severe weather in September 1968 when flooding caused by torrential rain storms, resulted in a landslide demolishing part of a house in Garlands Road. As the waters spread, canoes were used and police had to wade up to their waists to rescue elderly people from their homes. Apart from bad weather, fire was the cause of several catastrophies in the sixties and the worst was undoubtedly the destruction of the Surrey Mirror building in Ladbroke Road. Starting in the middle of the night, flames shot through the roof and by dawn the once-proud landmark was a smouldering ruin. Despite the damage the paper still appeared in the shops the following Friday, thereby up-holding an unblemished record of, "delivering the goods no matter what the difficulty". And delivering the goods was a principle they continued to uphold, particularly regarding the re-development proposals which received banner headlines in 1963.

"SETTLING THE FUTURE TOWN CENTRE
Redhill is being strangled the planners declare
RE-DEVELOP NOW - OR DIE"

And in July several days were occupied by a public inquiry into the Redhill Development Plan. Action would have to be taken and decisions made soon. As C.W. Brightwell, Deputy Town Clerk asserted;

"The proposals affecting the very existence of the eastern half of the Borough for the next few decades, were of vital concern to the Council. Unless development was tackled urgently and with imagination, either effective control over re-development would be lost for ever, or the town would stagnate, decay and die".

Despite a lack of Government ministerial blessing for the plan, some re-development did proceed and the new Redstone Secondary School was opened in September. In the private sector there was further progress too, when a hall was built as an extension to the British Legion Club premises in Clarendon Road. But the saga of closures continued, as Kennards ceased trading in the High Street after sixteen years. And in October it was announced that British Industrial Sand, which had evolved from the Standard Brick Company of Holmethorpe, was to merge with General Refractories.

Though the problems of the town continued to be the major news item, the Council were determined to celebrate their centenary. And this they did in grand style with numerous events throughout the year, even ensuring that the works of Samuel Palmer and John Linnell were suitably exhibited. In January the County Cross Country Championships attracted a big entry, while at the Market Hall the East Surrey Operatic Society gave a fine performance of Merrie England. But the Redhill and Reigate Round Table's Donkey Derby and Fete at the Memorial Sports Ground, was considered by many to have been "the best yet". In fact there were attractions for everyone, not least the centenary carnival procession which was watched by an estimated crowd of 50,000.

If the sixties had been dominated by deliberations over the town centre, the seventies were little different, though by now there was a reluctant acceptance of the inevitable. An acceptance that whatever plans were eventually approved, Redhill would be changed beyond all recognition. Nothing new in a town that had undergone infinite changes since its inception, only this time the eventual "new look" would be far more dramatic.

The seventies also brought an inevitable increase in the cost of living, which affected everyone and was reflected in prices over a broad front. But at least "just looking" cost nothing and this included the Veteran Car Rally, one of the most popular events on the Redhill calendar. And not just popular in the seventies, for the London to Brighton Rally remains today a spectacle enjoyed by young and old alike. As the robust old cars struggle up the Brighton Road to The Cutting, perhaps the ghost of Brown is lurking about wishing he could help, as he did with the coaches so many years ago. But he need not worry, for there are other helpers and among them Eddie and Mary Waller, who live on the brow of the hill. As Mary puts it;

> "I think we must have unconsciously continued this tradition of helping people up the hill, because every year Eddie goes out with water and we have them in here, using the toilets sometimes!"

But though the cost of living was affecting everyone and the way they shopped, many people were genuinely concerned by the gradual disappearance of small shopkeepers. For so long they had been part of Redhill's commercial development, but now the arrival of supermarkets had dealt them a death blow. Some managed to survive like the Kiwi Store in Earlswood, but most were unable to compete and gradually went out of business over the next decade and a half. In many areas of Redhill it was an end of the old world village atmosphere; and more significantly of the shops that were meeting-places for daily 'housewife' gossip. For it was this village atmosphere which prompted one-newly arrived shopkeeper in Meadvale to remark;

> ' I've lived in six countries and this is the loveliest village I've seen. The people are so friendly''.

And this was true also of a keen-eyed milkman, who, in November 1977, saved the life of a sick pensioner when he noticed his milk had not been collected. But while this caring milkman was carrying out his good deed, an Irishman was, as one newspaper unwittingly reported, "thricking three Redhill banks into handing over hundreds of pounds".

For most people the year was memorable for the Queen's Silver Jubilee celebrations, which Redhill laid on in red carpet style. Apart from special church services, there was a jubilee fun day organised by the Lions Club at St. Nicholas School and a sports and tattoo event at the Memorial Sports Ground. And all over Redhill children joined in the fun with traditional street parties. But there was also fun to be had at Busby's drag party, when popular Capital Radio DJ Kenny Everett made an appearance. Reporting the occasion the Surrey Mirror concluded;

> "...In between throwing albums and singles to the crowd like confetti, he kissed the boys and made them laugh ....then kissed the girls and made them sigh. The event staged by the Railway Inn in Earlswood, in aid of muscular dystrophy, raised about £800".

And money was in the news in April, when the final plans for Redhill's multi-million pound hospital were unveiled, after more than fifteen years on the drawing-board. While some viewed the plans, others went along to watch England cricket star John Edrich open the nurses training centre at Redhill General Hospital.

Though the cost of living continued to be a problem, an increasing number of shoppers were now using supermarkets as a means of budgetting. In September prices were still reasonably stable, with potatoes at 1p a lb and a white cabbage at 3p a lb. But so, too, was drink which, despite tax increases, encouraged customers to stock up early for Christmas with whisky at £4.19 and vodka at £3.99 a bottle. However, the best value remained in the property market as Gascoigne Pees were quick to advertise;

> "An extremely well-modernised older style semi-detached house, offers gas central heating, part double glazing, entrance hall, lounge, dining room, kitchen, downstairs cloakroom, cellars, 4 bedrooms, bathroom, garden. Close to Town centre £15,450 freehold".

As the decade drew to a close arsonists were busy at work and took pleasure in March, by setting fire to the boathouse at Earlswood lakes. A few weeks later they were striking matches again, this time on the other side of the Common, completely destroying the Redhill Cricket Club pavilion. A new boatouse and tea kiosk were built at a cost of £70,000 and for a few years, the facilities were enjoyed by large crowds at weekends. But seeing people enjoying themselves is not part of the arsonist's code of life. In 1985 they struck again at dead of night and by the morning light, all that remained was a pile of ashes and a few blackened upright timbers.

But the year ended on a happier note, when the Surrey Mirror celebrated its centenary with a special edition. On the front page was a message from Her Majesty the Queen;

> "TO THE EDITOR
> I sincerely thank you and the staff of the Surrey Mirror for your kind message of loyal greetings, sent on the occasion of the newspaper's centenary. I send warmest good wishes to the readers and to all those associated with the production of the paper on this notable occasion".

In 1982 after a long and often bitter fight, the old Market Hall lost its bid for survival and the demolition men moved in. Five years later at 11am on 21st April 1987, HRH The Duke of Gloucester arrived to officially open the new Warwick Quadrant, by unveiling a plaque. It was the culmination of years of planning and discussions which had often been heated, as traditionalists argued for the Victorian character of the town centre to be retained. But most agreed that the run-down area of shops and houses had to go and sadly, too, the Market Hall.

Although the re-development was delayed until 1982, the scheme was revised and work began on site in October of the following year. Development was undertaken by the Norwich Union Insurance Group, in partnership with

Surrey County Council and the Borough Council. On the north east section of the site, an imposing red-bricked office block began to take shape, soon to be the new headquarters of Lombard North Central. Yet another example of the confidence the business world had in the town. The contractors, John Mowlem & Co. Plc, handed over the retail element of the complex in time for fitting out and trading before Christmas 1985. Here the giant supermarket of Sainsburys occupied a major section of the ground level, almost in sight of its pre-war premises in Station Road. Upstairs the library and the magnificent Harlequin Theatre added new life to the town centre, after the dusty months of demolition and construction. Soon other occupants arrived, offering a variety of products and services. Macdonalds, facing across the roundabout to the station, where shoppers could munch away and contemplate shopping around the corner for hi-fi, cards, shoes, books or toothpaste; Abbey National, where a prudent withdrawal would secure the holiday bargain on offer at Hogg Robinson next door; or perhaps just browse in Clintons and Fourbuoys, before making a decision to buy that hi-fi at Currys; a truly striking complex, retaining within its name the nostalgia of the nineteenth century connection, yet designed as the first stage of a re-vitalised Redhill.

And it was a year for other business expansion, as the giant Holmethorpe Industrial Estate attracted new skills and expertise, to add to Redhill's growing commercial reputation. A year which also saw Hockley Holdings acquire the old railway goods yard in Hooley Lane and establish its industrial centre. Here just after the war corn and timber merchants had used the site, while at one time, railway horses had been stabled in one of the original buildings now used by a joinery company. And over the years this mini-industrial estate has grown, accommodating modern versions of the cottage industries that were such an important part of Redhill's early days.

But there were other important developments too and not least among them, the opening of the New East Surrey Hospital near Whitebushes. Now at last there was a first-class hospital, that could cater for a much wider area outside the Borough. But catering for recreational needs within the Borough was also important. And this was finally recognised with the opening in 1984 of Donyngs Recreation Centre. Deriving its name from the old mansion nearby, the Centre was immensely popular from the start, particularly amongst the younger members of the community. The swimming pool complex was an obvious attraction, but the other facilities offered were designed to cater for a wide variety of tastes. Though not the kind of tastes a young postman had in mind, when he offered to raise money for charity. Setting out to eat thirty sausages in one sitting, he had devoured twelve of the eight-inch bangers, when his stomach decided enough was enough.

"It was 'orrible", he said. "They tasted quite nice at first, but after a few I felt worse and worse. I was feeling so ill there was no way I could make it".

But despite his failure in front of an excited crowd at the Flying Scud, his efforts did raise money for the Royal National Lifeboat Institution.

As the eighties drew to a close and people basked in the warmth of summer sunshine, the minds of some dwelt for a while on a decade that had seen momentous changes. Not just the structural changes to the town centre, but the radical changes which had altered society and the way of living. Changes which had seen growing unemployment and the first signs of a weakening local housing market. No different from elsewhere in the country, but nonetheless hard to accept when its one's home town. But apart from the changes, perhaps the event which remains sharpest in people's memories, is the night of the Great Storm and the damage it caused in Redhill and the south of England.

Packing winds of hurricane strength, it struck in the early hours of Friday 17th October 1987 and left a trail of utter devastation in its wake. Nothing was sacred; oak trees that had stood from before the birth of the town, were uprooted like matchsticks and sent crashing onto houses and across roads. Throughout the darkness of the night, chimney stacks were torn down and roof tiles sent scything through the air. In Woodlands Road a man peering out of his front door, narrowly missed being de-capitated when a slate embedded itself a good six inches in his lawn. Such was the force and fury, that cars were bowled over and wooden fences sent flying into oblivion.

Despite a tragic loss of life elsewhere in the South, Redhill had few casualties, apart from cuts and bruises sustained during the clearing -up process. As Paul Alderson of The East Surrey Health Authority commented;

"The bottom line is that we were fortunate. If this had happened during the day instead of at dead of night, God knows how many casualties we would have had. I have no doubt out mortuary would have been full".

Long after memories have faded and witnesses passed on, the shattered trunks and strangely angled trees on the Commons, will still remain for future generations to see.

As the clearing up process began the "cowboys" arrived, sharp as ever to "cash in on a good thing". They were of many diverse occupations, but in particular presenting themselves as qualified Tree Surgeons, armed with chain saws. Removing a tree blocking a driveway was cheap at £100, compared to the "qualified" roofers who extracted £150 from a pensioner in Garlands Road, for replacing six roof tiles.

Not the way the pioneer entrepeneurs of Redhill would have conducted business; and certainly not the charitable spirit of helping, that is so characteristic of Redhill's people. Thankfully they are the exceptions, for Redhill is, and hopefully always will, remain a caring community.

REDHILL CINEMAS

FOR THE DISCRIMINATING PICTURE-GOER.

Programmes.

THE PAVILION.

July 13th—MARGARET SULLAVAN in Ursula Parrott's famous story—"NEXT TIME WE LIVE."
JACK HOLT in "DANGEROUS WATERS," with Robert Armstrong and Grace Bradley.

July 20th—FRED ASTAIRE and GINGER ROGERS in "TOP HAT." Lyrics and music by Irving Berlin.
"EVERY SATURDAY NIGHT," with JUNE LANG, JED PROUTY and Spring Byington.

July 27th—VICTOR McLAGLEN in "THE INFORMER." Magnificent acting that won last year's Gold Medal in a thrilling drama of Ireland during the late Rebellion.
DONALD COOK and Evalyn Knapp in "CONFIDENTIAL."

August 3rd—FRED ASTAIRE and GINGER ROGERS in "FOLLOW THE FLEET," with Randolph Scott.
"THE VIRGINIA JUDGE," with WALTER C. KELLY.

August 10th—WILL HAY in his Latest Picture, "WHERE THERE'S A WILL."
"TWICE BRANDED," with Robert Rendel and Lucille Lisle.

THE PICTURE HOUSE.

July 13th—EDWARD ARNOLD in "REMEMBER LAST NIGHT," with Constance Cummings and Robert Young.
EDMUND LOWE in "KING SOLOMON OF BROADWAY."

July 20th—EDMUND LOWE in "THE GREAT IMPERSONATION." From the pen of the world's most celebrated mystery author E. Phillips Oppenheim.
"THE LAST OF THE PAGANS"—a page torn from the History of the South Sea Islands.

July 27th—PAT O'BRIEN, JEAN MUIR and Frank McHugh in "STARS OVER BROADWAY."
"MR. COHEN TAKES A WALK," with Paul Graetz and Chili Bouchier.

August 3rd—WARNER OLAND in "CHARLIE CHAN'S SECRET."
JOAN BLONDELL and GLENDA FARRELL in "MISS PACIFIC FLEET," with Allen Jenkins.

August 10th—CHESTER MORRIS, LEWIS STONE and WALTER BRENNAN in "THREE GODFATHERS." From the novel by Peter B. Kyne.
ARLINE JUDGE and MONA BARRIE in "HERE COMES TROUBLE," with Paul Kelly.

Inset for the REIGATE & REDHILL OBSERVER.

S. C. Jennings & Sons, Ltd., Redhill.

The Roundabout, Earlswood Common.
(courtesy E. Freeman)

The Warwick Hotel which stood on the site
of Safeways. It and other buildings were
demolished when Queensway was constructed.
(courtesy E. Freeman)

Aerial view of Linkfield Corner and adjacent roads. (courtesy Redhill Library)

Redhill Town Centre c.1950
(courtesy Redhill Library)

The old stable, Hockley Industrial Centre
(courtesy C. McGregor)

The Church Lads Brigade
marching along Station Road c.1952
(courtesy Mrs R.J. Uwins)

Brighton Road at the junction with
Garlands Road and Hooley Lane, 1967
(courtesy Redhill Library)

THE BELFRY

STATION ROAD LEVEL SHOPPING

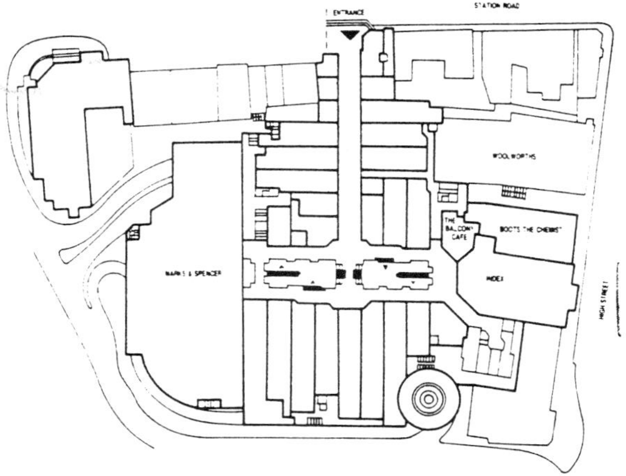

UNITS: Marks & Spencer (First Floor)
Gamleys (Toys)
Evans
Seeboard
Stationery Plus
Index
Sportif (Intersport)
The Card Company
Thorntons
The Linen Shop
Athena
Supercuts
Cheltenham & Gloucester Building Society
Amanda Howard
The Body Shop
Törq
Kids Carnival
The Balcony Café

HIGH STREET LEVEL SHOPPING

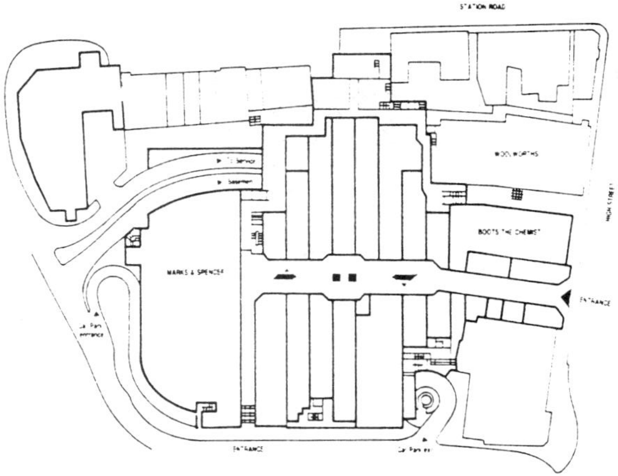

UNITS: Marks & Spencer (Ground Floor)
Dorothy Perkins
Our Price
Burton (including Champion Sport)
Dixons
Optional Extras
WH Smith
Clothes Rail
H Samuel
Boots the Chemist
Etam
Principles
Richards
Clarks

The Harlequin Theatre auditorium
(courtesy Harlequin Theatre)

On 15 October 1991 all roads literally led to Redhill, when the Belfry Shopping Centre opened its doors for the first time. The Surrey Mirror's 'Mum in a Million' Sian Cumins, had the honour of performing the official opening assisted by celebrity guest Joanna Lumley. Thousands of people flocked to the opening and within a few hours, it was estimated that 15,000 had visited the Centre. (courtesy Surrey Mirror)

The generosity of Redhill residents was never more evident than when the appeal for Bosnia was launched. On 17 April 1993 members of the Bosnia Family Aid Appeal were outside Sainsburys, asking people to part with some of their food to be sent to the needy in the war-torn country. (courtesy Surrey Mirror)

Earlswood Nursery School raised over £100 for Comic Relief when they held a non-uniform day in March 1993. The children had to pay a minimum of 10p and the teachers who had to wear school uniforms, also made donations to the worth-while cause. (courtesy Surrey Mirror)

In May 1992 work to give a new lease of life to the play area at Fairfax Avenue, got off to a flying start when the Mayor and Mayoress Eddie and Mary Waller gave a helping hand. Largely due to the efforts of local resident Mrs Hardy McBride and funds from the Council, the children could look forward to a variety of facilities. But it was the children themselves who had a say in deciding what was needed. As Mrs McBride remarked; "It's all the work of the children. I don't want any of the glory taken away from those kids".
(courtesy Surrey Mirror)

Adventurous pupils gathered at St. Bede's School in January 1993, to be presented with their awards for completing the Duke of Edinburgh's Scheme. (courtesy Surrey Mirror)

The popularity of the Harlequin Theatre's varied programme of events, was clearly demonstrated when a capacity "younger generation" went wild to the sounds of the local pop group Spanglehead. As one reporter commented, "it won't be long before they receive the recognition they deserve in the industry." (courtesy Surrey Mirror)

The High Street - Christmas 1992

Redhill Rotary Club president Harry Plumridge handed a cheque for £2400 to Pauline Stobhard at Centenary House. It was one of the many fund raising efforts made towards the cost of refurbishing the Centre in Warwick Road.
(courtesy Surrey Mirror)

Chapter 11
TOWARDS THE MILLENNIUM

The story is almost told and yet it is not completely told. It never will be; not even a single day of Redhill's story could ever be told in its entirety. Except perhaps the major events or issues of the day recorded in the media. But then they are only part of the story as Aubrey, Ridgeway, Hooper and the other great historians of the past would agree. True they recorded events, but it was about life and people and "happenings" in their time that was important; a kaleidoscope of historical snapshots which only their pens could record.

But here within these pages as the millennium approaches, people and their "happenings" have been recorded in photographs as well as the written word. Perhaps but a few; never the complete story, but nonetheless a record of the present and the past; a legacy of historical snapshots for future generations to digest.

"Happenings", such as the highly successful "Raise the Roof" appeal for St. John's Church, which officially closed in March 1992 having reached £111,000. The appeal was launched after the church suffered extensive damage to its roof in the Great Gale of January 25th 1990. Eightyfive mile an hour winds stripped over 600 slates from the main roof, aisle and vestry roofs, exposing rotten batons underneath. The money was raised in a variety of ways including fetes, jumble sales, an 'antique roadshow' style auction and a grand "Messiah" concert held in the church. But perhaps the most remarkable fund raising effort was the feat of 82 year old Leslie Quinton of Earlswood. He raised a total of £2000 by climbing Mount Snowdon, a height of 3650 feet.

However, charity was not in evidence on New Year's Eve 1993. For as revellers saw in the New Year in traditional style, the less law-abiding members of the community were hard at work. In the High Street Corals received a visit which relieved them of over £5000, in what police described as "a totally professional job". Meanwhile, in other areas of the Borough figurines, bicycles and coins from unprotected meters were fair game for nimble fingers. All in a night's work it could be said but it was impossible for the police to be everywhere, particularly when they were on the lookout for drunken drivers. And in this excercise they made some arrests, including that of one young man who, after crashing his car in the Brighton Road, told them he was Frank Bruno.

Perhaps not a great event to include in Redhill's story, but a "happening" nonetheless, as the town moved into its 150th year. Nor can it be said that a casual walk to town in 1994 is a major event of historical importance. But to record it is important, for it is descriptive of the Redhill of today, as T.R. Hooper's writings were of Linkfield Street in 1854.

The eloquence of Hooper's description of his arrival in Redhill in 1854 is difficult, if not impossible to match. There can of course be no comparison, for he was a product of an age of horses and carriages and of grand houses set back in majestic lawns, from tree-lined avenues. And beyond the cottages of Linkfield Street, the meadows and tree-covered slopes of Redhill Common, a constant sea of movement. Nature's movement; of grazing cows and myriads of butterflies, dancing and weaving amidst the coppices. Of rabbits too, eyes and ears alert, peering through the lush blades of gently swaying grass. And high above in the trees the continuous chorus of birds, no roar of traffic here to drown their songs. A scene of nineteenth century tranquillity; easy to describe; easy for the words of eloquence to flow,

But that is of another age long gone and no way descriptive of a walk to town today. For here, starting from the top of Brighton Road, is a steady accompaniment of roaring traffic, almost to the very heart of town. A snake-like procession of cars, lorries, vans and weaving motorbikes; a rising crescendo of noise and vibration.

A glance across the road to the New Inn now boarded-up, paint flaking from grimy window frames. Inside the gathering cobwebs of time, collecting dust amongst the ghostly memories of a bygone age, when pints were drawn for thirsty travellers. Or drawn perhaps for the former occupants of the nearby Victorian terrace, now the home of Mortons The Padlock and the vets surgery. But this incessant noise of engines and squeaking brakes affords no time for reflection. Nor do the rising clouds of exhaust fumes encourage one to linger, as Hooper would have done in Linkfield Street those years ago. Nothing in common, except perhaps the clear blue sky above and the dazzling sunshine of an early February morning.

On the right a hoarding, hiding the churned-up ground that once held the sturdy structure of the Noah's Ark. While beside it a few forlorn cottages, once part of a greater terrace of shops and houses. And across from here the showrooms of Bakers offering cars for the modern traveller, on the very site that John Moody, wheelwright, built coaches and carts 150 years ago.

At No. 82 the Greyhound pub now closed but scheduled to re-open. And further along more boarded buildings, once thriving shops and now in sad decay; a prime site for development with the neighbouring plot at Brook Road. A pause at the kerb, to avoid being run down by a modern 'chariot', then quick march across Brook Road to the BP Service Station on the other corner. Here halfway down the Brighton Road the familiar sounds grow louder, as just beyond a vast site is made ready for the new occupants, Halfords and Pet City. A virtual army of builders, oblivious to the hammering diggers and the mud and dust around them. An accepted resignation etched on the face of a passing pedestrian, as he picks his way through the maze of machinery. For he and the others have seen it all before, as did their forefathers, the all-familiar building scene that has been so much part of Redhill's history. Another glance, this time across the spacious forecourt and in the centre, Redhill's merry brook encased in a concrete culvert. Across the road more evidence of the building boom of recent years. Here between two derelict sites stand Furness Withy and Forum House, typical red-bricked office palaces of glass and steel, that are the hallmark of Redhill's modern architecture.

Passing now the plush headquarters of Hall & Co., a landmark on the corner of Reading Arch Road. A road which leads to a mini estate of small businesses, where once the giant gasworks stretched from the railway to the Brighton Road. And on its opposite corner the Henlys Ford of Redhill complex, behind which are Taylor Autos, Watling Tyres and Humphreys and Willis. But there are other types of businesses across the Brighton Road. A parade of narrow terraced shops to delight the stomachs of the Take-Away fraternity; Tong Fung, Redhill Kebab House and Southern Fried Chicken and alongside them, to relieve parched throats, Unwins and the Garlands public house.

Another pause on the kerb, waiting for the miracle of a break in the stream of traffic. Not worth dicing with death and ending up beneath the wheels of a snarling juggernaut. Better to wait patiently, like the little old lady with her shopping trolley on the opposite side; expressionless, accepting the muddy spray from uncaring motorists.

And now at last the chance to cross; keen glances right and left; swift steps to the safety of the pavement. Here at the bottom of Grove Hill Road the furnishing store of Bucklands, on the same site they have occupied since the turn of the century. More traffic now beneath the Reading Arch Bridge, as the Brighton Road merges with the High Street. A slight incline of the pavement and above it the Bridge Gate office block, where once the faithful came to worship at St. Joseph's Church. And below this elevated walkway, a gently sloping bank of greenery and floral colour to the road.

The High Street, with Kingsway House and Berkeley House on either side, the only section that remains open to one-way traffic until it reaches Cromwell Road. Here on the corner, The Office public house and, in former days Crocks, still bears a certain Victorian grandeur at the entrance to the pedestrian precinct. No traffic here, just people and an avenue of shops and offices of every kind. To the left Millets, Halifax, Relate and across from them Argus and the closed -down Dewhurst premises, a victim of recessionary times. But no obvious hint of this today, in the bustling pedestrian thoroughfare that is the High Street. For this is market day; stalls 'cheek and jowl' along its length; vast throngs digging deep into wallets and purses. A pulsating High Street of purchasers and sellers; a steady flow of shoppers through the glass doors of the Belfry, to the glittering stores within.

And towards the old Crossroads, Boots, Woolworths, the Woolwich and finally the Wheatsheaf. Here outside the crowds are dense, a constant movement of young and old. Some edging along Station Road towards Macdonalds; others stopping briefly enticed by the wafting smells of the hot-dog stand. And in the centre clutching papers, a lone figure, voice raised, entreating the passer-by to "help the homeless".

This, then, is the hub of the town as it has been from the beginning. The focal point from which it has stretched and grown, changed and changed again. And probably will do so again, for Redhill knows no other way.

Canadian ex-servicemen on parade outside Canada Hall, Merstham, which they built in 1941 after German bombs had destroyed the church and vicarage.(courtesy Surrey Mirror)

Danny Canning, chairman of the Redhill 150 Committee, receiving the keys of a Mini Sprite from Lombard North Central Chief Executive, Brian Carte. The car was the prize in the lottery held in 1994 by Redhill 150, in aid of local charities.

Redhill Station 150 years on

APPENDIX 1

REDHILL SNIPPETS

During the course of my research, I came across the names of a number of people associated with Redhill's past who have given their names to streets and roads. There was also a considerable amount of other information I was unable to include in the narrative of this book. All of these Snippets are relevant to The Redhill Story and I have therefore, included them here in chronological order.

GATTON - literally means Goats Farm (Anglo-Saxon)
MERSTHAM - Ham is the Anglo-Saxon word for village and taken together, Merstham means literally, 'at the horse enclosure'. However, a Medieval interpretation is 'stone house by the mere or marsh'.
CHART or CHURT - means sandy, scrubby heathland.
EARLSWOOD - also known as Erleswode around 1500 and later as Aleswood.
HOLEAGH(HOOLEY) - meaning woodland or clearing in the hollow.
MEADVALE - known in the 19th century as Mead Hole. The name means meadowland hollow. In Victorian times the village had two butchers, a baker, a draper, a tailor and a grocer's shop. The first school to be opened was held in the village hall. Parents had to pay one penny a week for each child. At the beginning of the 19th century, there was a tanyard adjoining Earlswood Common at the entrance to Meadvale. Clarence Walk was once known as Cat Walk.
GARLANDS - probably so named after John Gerlaund who lived in the district in 1255.
BRAMBLETYE PARK ROAD - formerly was a farm road known as Hooley Road, which ran through the land belonging to Hooley Farm.
WIGGEY - also known as Wiggie - Wygehaye - Wiggy
REIGATE CAVES - the caves beneath the town and surrounding area, were originally dug to mine hearthstone and firestone. Hearthstone was used to whiten hearths and stone floors. Firestone acquired its name on

account of the resistance of the bricks to heat and were widely used in the building trade.

PRICE'S LANE - named after William Price of Woodhatch. He was a friend and supporter of St. John's School from its early days. A schoolroom and master's house were later erected in his memory, after his death in 1858.

ST. JOHNS - Near the 'Little London' cottages was Crockerty Well, which provided the local water supply. It is uncertain how the well got its name. This was the focal point for the local community in the early 1800's, where old and young alike gathered to gossip.

WOODLANDS ROAD - formerly meadow-land called Woodlands belonging to the Manor of Hooley. In the 18th century it was farmed by an Edward Heath.

HIGH TREES - named after the tall elm trees which once grew on the hill. In 1890 the property was owned by M. Marcus and included a model farm breeding Jersey cattle.

GURNEY, H.E. - A well-known 19th century banker. The Redhill brook is often referred to as Gurney's Brook. Gurney's Close has been named after him.

MOSTYN TERRACE - named after Lady Mostyn who lived in Hooley Lane and was the principal benefactor of St. Joseph's Church.

RENNIE TERRACE - bears the name of Sir John Rennie, the engineer who designed the London, Brighton & South Coast Railway.

CORMONGERS LANE - The lane derives its name from a family called Cornmongers who lived in the area in the 16th century.

HATCHLANDS ROAD - originally known as Workhouse Lane, it was renamed in 1863 after an old farm in the area. Adjacent, was another farm called Fengates. In fact in the early 19th century the whole area consisted of farms and smallholdings. For some years, the houses in Charman and Fengates roads used to possess in their gardens, the remains of farm watering wells.

MURDER - In 1824 a young lad of 14 was robbed and murdered on Earlswood Common and his body thrown into the New Pond. About three weeks later it was found washed ashore, but the murderers were never caught.

ROYAL EARLSWOOD HOSPITAL - In 1869 the foundation stone of the new wing was laid by the Prince and Princess of Wales. It was a grand occasion and faithfully recorded by Mrs Grece in her diary;

> "June 28th 1869 - A fine day and a gay one at the Asylum. The Prince of Wales and the Princess were there and hundreds of people besides. Royalty the principal attraction. The Prince placed the foundation stone of the new wing".

LAMPLIGHTERS - Though some lamplighters used horses, most would be seen running from lamp-post to lamp-post in the town before it got dark. Certainly they would have been fast and fit. Unwittingly, they passed another expression into the English language viz., when anyone asked to deliver an urgent message was told to "run like a lamplighter".

INDUSTRY - the first industrial exhibition held in Redhill was in 1874.

MAIDS - In the 1870's maids worked from 6am until 10pm for a few shillings a week. Though the hours were long the jobs were much sought after, as accommodation and food were provided.

ST. MATTHEW'S BOY' SCHOOL - was built in 1868.

ST. JOHN'S CHURCH - The longest-serving vicar was Rev H. Gosse from 1846-1882.

FOWLE, HENRY - was one of the tradesmen keen to have a Borough Council. He was a watchmaker by trade and provided the Mayor's chain of office at almost cost price.

ST. PAUL'S CHURCH - was built in 1902.

CONGREGATIONAL CHURCH - was built in Chapel Road in 1862.

WESLEYAN CHAPEL - was built in Woodlands Road in 1878.

HOOLEY LANE STATION - The stationmaster's house was on the east side of the tracks at No. 17 Hooley Lane, but has since been demolished.

THE REDHILL SOCIETY OF INSTRUMENTALISTS - was founded in 1891 and is one of the oldest musical societies in existence in the country.

SANITATION - It was common prior to proper sanitation, for the contents of chamber pots to be thrown into the back garden or yard. This frequently happened close to wells which provided drinking water. In the towns this action caused widespread diseases.

REDHILL BAPTIST BAND OF HOPE - the organisation was formed as a temperance movement in the Victorian era, to combat the ever-increasing drink problem. Whole families, including children, spent most of their money in gin houses.

RAILWAY FARES - in 1884 a 3rd class return fare from Redhill to Horley was 10d.

POPULATION - in 1895 the population of Redhill was 13,500.

EAST SURREY COLLEGE - can trace its origins back to the old Redhill Technical College which opened in 1895. Until it was demolished in recent years, the building fronted Redstone Hill between Noke Drive and Cavendish Road.

REES ROAD - was laid out by James Rees, Redhill's first estate agent. It ran from the High Street to the left of where Boots the Chemists are today and came out in Station Road just to the right of the Belfry entrance.

ATHENAEUM PRINTING WORKS - stood back from the Brighton Road on the site now occupied by Furness House.

GEORGE ELIOT - the writer, was the pseudonym of Mary Ann (Marion) Evans who lived from 1819-1880. Best known for her novel Middlemarch, she lived for a period in The Cottage, Earlswood Common opposite the old Workhouse. During this time she wrote Daniel Deronda, which was published in instalments between 1874 and 1876 and was her last great novel.

COSTAR'S HILL - The stretch of Pendleton Road from the Brighton Road to Sandpit Lane. It was so-called after the Costar family who lived at "Woodlands", a large house and grounds which stood near the junction of Brighton and Pendleton roads, on what is now Pendleton Close.

THE ROUNDABOUT - a group of cottages that once stood on Earlswood Common close to the New Pond.

HOLY TRINITY CHURCH - was consecrated in 1903 and became a parish church in 1907.

COLMAN INSTITUTE - was opened in 1904. It was a gift to the town by Sir Jeremiah Colman of Gatton and included a working-men's club.

CHAMBER OF COMMERCE - one of the founder trustees was Arthur Wood, who established a pianoforte business in the town in the late nineteen hundreds.

REES, LEONARD - was the architect of the Pavilion Cinema (1912). He was also a founder-member of the Chamber of Commerce.

AIRSHIP - In July 1913 an airship belonging to the Royal Flying Corps was forced to make an emergency landing near Mason's Bridge, because of a damaged rudder. The unexpected visitor attracted large crowds who flocked to the farmer's field, including hoardes of school children.

BRITISH WAX REFINING CO. LTD. - started business in 1914 from premises in Lower Bridge Road. In 1917 the company moved to St. John's Road to a site behind Taylors the car dealers.

REDHILL FOOTBALL CLUB - was founded during the season 1894/95.

FIRE BRIGADE - the manuals were replaced in 1924 with the purchase of a second motor appliance.

THE ROTARY CLUB OF REDHILL - was founded in 1928.

TELEPHONE - The Redhill Telephone exchange opened in 1930, taking over from the small exchange originally set up in Rees's house in Chapel Road.

RAILWAY FARES - In 1936/7 a 3-month season ticket (3rd class) from Merstham to London cost £5.10/-.

ODEON CINEMA - now the Millionaire Club, was built in 1938.

REIGATE AND REDHILL CHORAL SOCIETY - was founded in 1941 and has been a part of the musical life of the town since that time. Today the Society holds concerts at the Harlequin Theatre and in local churches.

PERSONALITIES - in December 1949 Sir Lawrence Olivier paid a visit to Redhill and presented a prize to a young nurse, who had written a review of his film Hamlet.

LIBRARY - in August 1950 the Borough celebrated the centenary of the library service.

POLICE - in September 1950 the police moved from Reigate Town Hall to "Cherchefelle" in Chart Lane. In 1971 they moved to the present premises.

INNER WHEEL CLUB OF REDHILL - was founded in 1950 with Mrs Kerridge as its first President. The principal aims were of service to the community.

WARWICK HOTEL - was demolished in 1972.

SEA CADETS - celebrated their half-century in 1988, with a series of reunions, marches and tattoos throughout the year.

THE MILL HOUSE - at Salfords stands on the site of a former watermill.

MORTONS THE PADLOCK - at 141, Brighton Road, has been an ironmongers business for many years. In the early 1900's it traded under Gillams and, in later years, Cards and then LeFevre during the last war.

ST. MATTHEW'S CHURCH -in the great, hot summer of 1990, the official temperature on 3rd August reached 97 degrees Farenheit. This had a serious effect on the clock, which chimed 11 times at 5pm. On the same day in a garden in Earlswood, a temperature of 100 degrees was recorded for twenty minutes from 3pm.

CANADA ROAD - so-called on account of the Canadian troops stationed in Redhill during the war years

METHODIST CHURCH - and Centre were opened in 1993, as part of the overall re-development in the town centre.

YMCA - celebrated their 150th anniversary on 4th January 1994. At their sports and leisure complex in Earlswood 150 balloons were launched skywards, as young and old joined in a variety of activities free of charge.

PUBS

SUMMERS ARMS - at Linkfield Corner closed down in 1968. The last landlord, Dan Munro, allowed the toilets to be used by the general public, as they were the only ones between Redhill and Reigate. Between the pub and its rival The Red Lion, there were a row of cottages on the land now occupied by National Tyre and Autocare. At the turn of the century Linkfield Corner was a busy shopping centre and next to the Somers Arms, was Cutforth Brothers Brewery, now the site of Streat Motors. The Brewery supplied several pubs in Redhill and was originally founded by a Mr. Reffell, who later gave his name to the railway bridge.

THE ANCHOR - now Garlands, was originally built in 1865 but did not become a fully licensed premises until 1892.

THE GATTON - opened for business in 1951.

THE GLADSTONE ARMS - stood at the corner of Warwick Road in the late 1800's.

THE STATION HOTEL- now The Old Chestnut, Earlswood, was originally built in 1868.

THE BRITANNIA - another of the pubs built in the late 19th century. It was demolished in 1960.

NOAH'S ARK - was in Brighton Road close to the Sea Cadets. It was first a beer shop, before obtaining a full licence just after the last war. It closed in 1977.

THE QUEENS ARMS - was originally built in London Road around 1849. It was demolished in 1972.

THE ANGEL - in 1845 was in the postal district of Red Hill, when the licensee was a Mrs Pooley.

THE PLOUGH - an alehouse of the same name was originally on the site of the graveyard at St. Johns.

RED LION - at Linkfield Corner, has been altered considerably since it was built in 1760. It was originally a private residence.

RISING SUN - on White Post Hill was an alehouse from around 1750. It ceased trading in 1900.

APPENDIX 2

Eliza Cook, who was a well-known poet during the early part of the last century, stayed at the Waterhouse in Hooley Lane close to where Earlsbrook Road joins it now. Following the destruction of the old watermill and the necessity to divert the course of the brook for the construction of the railway, it is generally accepted that she was inspired to write her famous poem,

THE OLD MILL

And this is the old Mill-stream that ten years ago
was so fast in its current, so pure in its flow;
whose mineral waters would ripple and shine
with the glory and dash of a miniature Rhine?

Can this be its bed? I remember it well
when it sparkled like silver through meadow and dell;
when the pet-lamb reposed on its emerald side
and the minnow and perch darted swift through its tide.

Yes! here was the miller's house, peaceful abode!
where the flower-twined porch drew all eyes from the road;
where roses and jasmine embowered a door
that never was closed to the wayworn or poor.

Where the miller, God bless him! oft gave us a "dance",
and led off the ball with his soul in his glance;
Who, forgetting grey hairs, was as loud in his mirth
as the veriest youngsters that circled his hearth.

Blind Ralph was the only musician we had,
But his tunes -oh, such tunes - would make any heart glad!
"The Roast Beef of old England", and "Green grow the Rushes",
Woke our eyes brightest beams, and our cheeks' warmest flushes.

No lustre resplendent, its brilliancy shed,
But the wood fire blazed high and the board was well spread.
Our seats were undamasked, our partners were rough,
Yet, yet we are happy, and that was enough.

And here was the mill where we idled away
our holiday hours on a clear, summer day;
Where Roger, the miller's boy, lolled on a sack,
and chorused his song to the merry click-clack.

But lo! what rude sacrilege here hath been done;
the streamlet no longer purls in the sun;
Its course has been turned, and the desolate edge
is now mournfully covered with duck-weed and sedge.

The Mill is in ruins. No welcoming sound
in the mastiff's gruff bark and the wheels dashing round;
The house, too, untended - left to decay -
and the miller, long dead; all I loved passed away!

This play-place of childhood was graved on my heart
In rare Paradise Colours that must now depart;
the old Water-mill's gone, the fair vision is fled,
and I weep o'er its wreck as I do for the dead.

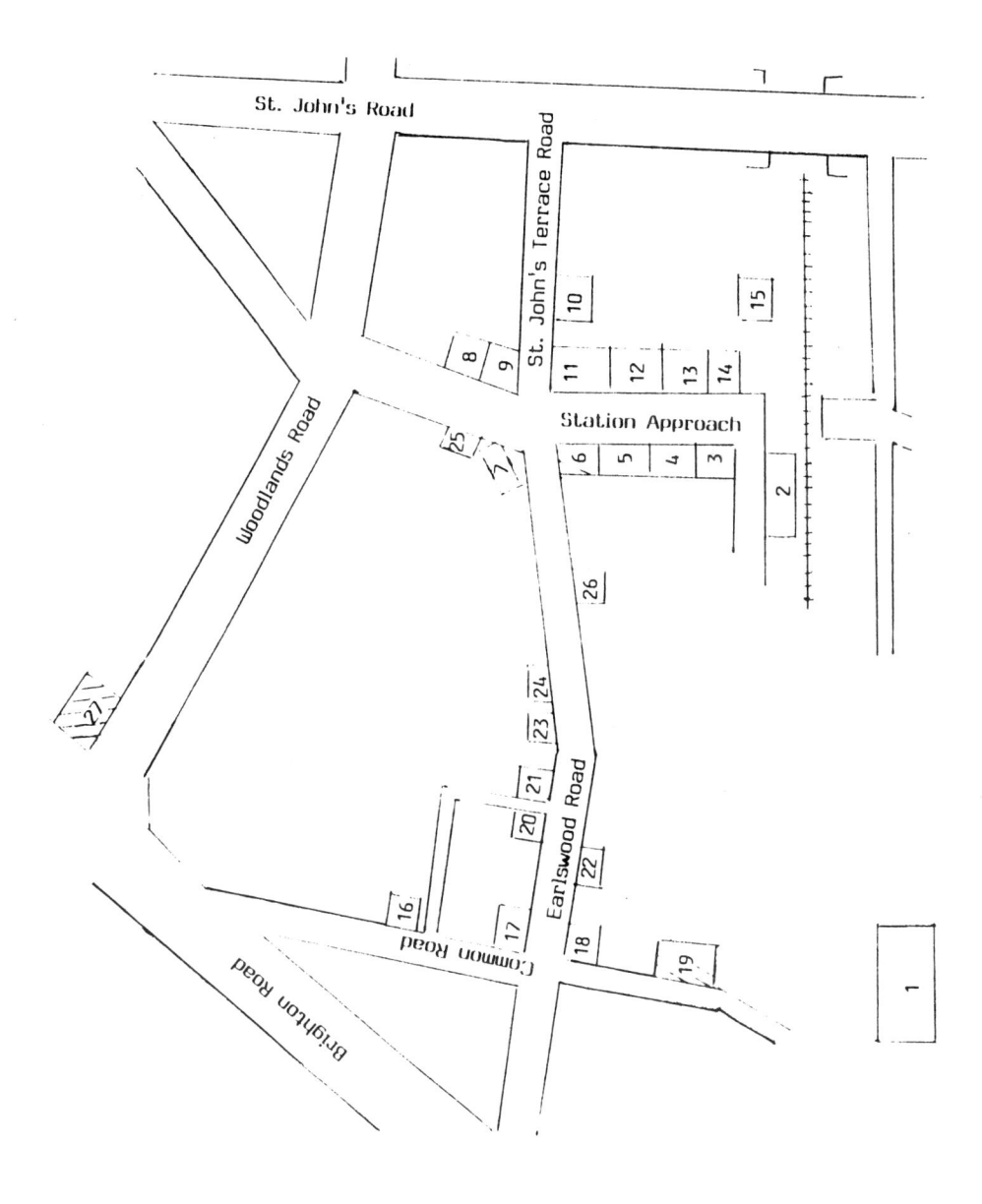

Map

St. John's Road

St. John's Terrace Road

Station Approach

Woodlands Road

Earlswood Road

Common Road

Brighton Road

Numbered locations: 1–27

APPENDIX 3

EARLSWOOD VILLAGE circa 1923
A Snapshot in time

1. The Royal Earlswood Hospital.
2. Earlswood Railway Station. There was living accommodation above the booking office.
3. Fred Watkins, butcher. In the mid-1930's the shop was taken over by Bellinghams the Reigate butchers. A Chinese Take-Away occupied the premises until 1988. It is now the Rushita Restaurant.
4. The bakery of Fred Sargent. Later this shop became a grocers and was taken over by a Mr Horwood. It is now the Take-Away part of Rushita.
5. Herbert Worth occupied the site as the village baker. The building is now vacant.
6. The Station Hotel. Landlord Patrick Whitty. His son Paddy later became landlord. In the twenties it only cost a few pence to buy a pint of beer, a pickled onion and a lump of cheese. The pub is now the Old Chestnut.
7. Dairy owned by Sidney Coomber until the mid-1930's. It is now a fish and chips Take-Away.
8. Fishmongers. Mr & Mrs A.H. Sheath. The shop closed in the 1960's.
9. In 1910 this was a general stores owned by Evelyn Saith's father H.J. Shergold. Prior to taking on the business, he fought against the Dervishes at Khartoum, Sudan and was one of the last people to see General Gordon alive. The shop later became a greengrocers and then reverted to a general store until it closed in the mid-1980's.
10. Dairy owned by Mr. Charlewood, now flats.
11. Grocery store and sub-post office. J.O. Hurdle was the owner until the mid-thirties when the Tisdall family bought the shop. The site is now occupied by a block of flats.
12. Chemist shop. A.E. Hamnett owned the shop until the late thirties when it was bought by Hockens and became a branch of their shop in Station Road, Redhill. The building has been converted into flats.

13. Drapery shop owned by two sisters the Misses Homewood until the mid-forties. In later years there were several owners. Today A1 Taxi Service operates from the premises, which owner Brian Habgood has converted into flats.
14. The ground floor was a newsagents selling tobacco, sweets and stationery. The shopkeeper was Miss S. Down. Upstairs the dentist William Woodward had his surgery. In the forties the owner was Vic Stone, the long distance athlete. In the seventies K.R. Jobanputra took over the business and has since extended it to an off-licence, general store and sub-post office.
15. Trowers Mill. It was severely damaged by fire in the midfifties and rebuilt. After being derelict for some years, the property was bought in 1993 and blocks of flats erected.
16. Confectionery shop owned by Mrs. Tranter. It is now a private residence.
17. Grocery shop owned by the Bashford family until the mid-sixties. It is now a private residence.
18. Confectionery shop owned by Jon Hewitt. It changed hands several times, passing from Johnsons to Walters to Rowlands. It is now the Earlswood Tandoori Take-Away.
19. The Railway Inn. Landlord, Charles Holder. In 1987 the name changed to The Albatross.
20. James Grove, Dairyman. with a yard through to Common Road. Harry Apps the builder carried on his business there in the 1950's. This and the succeeding old businesses are now all private residences.
21. Walter Baker, boot repairer.
22. Arthur King's old home at No. 86.
23. John Peters, mobile greengrocer. His donkeys grazed on the Common.
24. Robert Peters, chimney sweep.
25. Wholesale fruit and vegetable merchants, G.J. Wright Ltd., until the 1950's. Brake Bros. occupied the site until the mid-1980's when the property was converted into flats.
26. Nursery, greenhouses and cultivated beds around the house owned by William Hawker.
27. The Flying Scud public house.

ACKNOWLEDGEMENTS

It goes without saying, that no social history can be written without considerable help or encouragement from many people. Everyone who has helped me write THE REDHILL STORY, no matter how large or small a contribution they made, rightfully has an equal share in the finished product.

Much of my time was spent in research, over 400 hours in fact, 'thumbing' through some one hundred plus books in Redhill Library. At one stage I thought I had become part of the furniture and I think the staff did too! I am particularly indebted to Philip Morgan and his staff for putting up with me and the considerable help they gave, in allowing me access to their archives room. I would also like to make special mention of Evelyn Saith and "Jock" Mason, who lent me invaluable family papers and with whom I spent several hours reminiscing.

During my three months of research I made numerous phone calls and visits to many people, who had responded to my appeal in the Surrey Mirror. The end result was a wealth of photographs, material and personal memories, which hopefully have made THE REDHILL STORY come "alive". To all of them, a very big THANK YOU;

Jayne, for the loan of a typewriter, Mark Davison, Dorothy Tribe, Joyce Liddington, S.A. Field, Margaret Knight, Mr. Taylor, Mrs L. Gardiner, John Stoneman, Audrey Lyon, Jack Sales, D. Saith, Mrs. Savage, Jack Reeves, Bob Collins, Mary and Eddie Waller, Emma Currow of Reigate Priory Museum, Colin McGregor, P.T. Buckland, Brian Thomas, Mrs R.J. Uwins and my daughter Celine Dunne, who helped me with research. I am also grateful to Jim Chapman, Tom Jones and Tony Gowan, who gave me several informative snippets as we shared the odd ale.

Finally, I would like to thank Ernie Freeman for his major contribution in lending me photographs of old Redhill; my wife Rosemarie for her advance birthday present of a word processor which dramatically cut the work load and Danny Canning, for not only revealing to me the wonders of the machine, but being a constant source of encouragement throughout this project.

Nigel Dunne
Redhill
June 1994

BIBLIOGRAPHY

Green, F.E.	The Surrey Hills, Chatto Windus 1915
Hooper, Wilfred	Reigate: Its Story Through The Ages, Surrey Archaelogical Society 1945
Oppitz, Leslie	Surrey Railways Remembered, Countryside Books 1988
Davison, Mark & Currie, Ian	The Surrey Weather Book, Frosted Earth 1990
Aubrey, John	History of Surrey Vol 1 &4 First published 1718-19
Carter, E.F.	The Story of Redhill as a Railway Centre, The Holmesdale Press Ltd., 1955
Brayley, E.W.	History of Surrey, R.B. Ede, Dorking 1841
Phillips, Robt.	Geological, Historical & Topographical - Description of The Borough of Reigate, Phillips 1885
Wickham, Derek	Redhill - The Rise of a Railway Town in the Nineteenth Century A Study 1982
Ogilvy, J.S.	A Pilgrimage in Surrey, Routledge, London 1914
Morris, H.M.	The History of Merstham, 1971
Robinson, D.	Surrey Through The Century, Surrey County Council 1989
Dunne, Nigel	Arthur - The Story of Gunner Arthur King, Craigmore 1989
Surrey Federation of Womens Institutes,	Surrey Within Living Memory, Countryside Books 1992
Hunter, A.B. deM.	Gentlemen of Merstham and Gatton, The Book Guild Ltd. 1993
Sturt, George	A Small Boy in the Sixties, The Harvester Press 1977
Turner, Dennis	Surrey, George Phillip & Son Ltd. 1988
Trower, Arthur	Our Homestead, Sampson Low, Marston 1910
Palgrave, R.F.D.	Illustrated Handbook To Reigate, Reprinted Kohler

                             & Coombes 1973
                             Redhill Library Archives
                             Surrey Record Office Archives, Kingston
                             The Surrey Mirror
                             Reigate-Redhill News
                             The Independent
                             The William Mason papers and memorabilia
Ridgeway, William   History of Reigate
The History of St. John's Church, compiled by the Vicar and parishioners 1989
Focus on Social History, Stylus Press, Norfolk
McMillan, James   The Way it Changed 1951-1975, Wm. Kimber, London 1987
DuLake, Lawrence   The Doctor's Tale 1662-1975, DuLake 1977
Vigiles - Magazine of Surrey Fire Brigade

ABOUT THE AUTHOR

Nigel Dunne was born in Ireland in 1935. First joining an Irish bank, he later worked for the Hongkong and Shanghai Bank and spent 25 years in the Far East. His first book CLUB published in 1985, tells the social history of Hong Kong's premier sports club. This was followed by his biography ARTHUR, the story of Gunner Arthur King, a Redhill man. He has written several short stories and is currently working on a novel, before he tackles his next assignment, the History of Farnham Golf Club. He has recently completed his DIARIO DI COMPETA, an account of his experiences in a Spanish hill village.

Nigel lives in Redhill with his family, but tries to spend as much time as possible at his village cottage in Andalusia, Spain.